50 MORE WINNING BRIDGE TIPS

Ron Klinger's enormously successful *100 Winning Bridge Tips* was described by Alan Truscott, one of the all-time great names in bridge, as being 'crammed with nuggets of advice not available in other books'. This further selection of tips is aimed at players who want to improve further and has all the exciting and stimulating qualities of its celebrated predecessor.

No keen bridge player can afford not to read this book.

50 MORE WINNING BRIDGE TIPS

for the improving player

RON KLINGER

VICTOR GOLLANCZ
in association with
PETER CRAWLEY

First published in Great Britain 1996
in association with Peter Crawley
by Victor Gollancz
An imprint of the Cassell Group
Wellington House, 125 Strand, London WC2R 0BB

A catalogue record for this book
is available from the British Library

ISBN 0 575 06363 7

Typeset by Modern Bridge Publications, Sydney, Australia
Printed in Great Britain by
St Edmundsbury Press Ltd, Bury St Edmunds, Suffolk

CONTENTS

ACKNOWLEDGEMENT

I am indebted to Andrew Kambites who read the manuscript and made many useful and helpful suggestions. His acerbic wit notwithstanding, it is a pleasure to work with Andrew and to benefit from his ideas.

Ron Klinger

INTRODUCTION

100 Winning Bridge Tips was intended to form a solid foundation for a sound game of bridge. *50 More Winning Bridge Tips* was written in the hope that there are still players who are keen to improve, who will apply themselves, who will pore over the advice and apply it in their regular games. The tips are not meant primarily as entertainment but as a challenge to you (and your partner) to lift your game to higher peaks.

Many of the tips commence with bidding or play problems. The best way to approach these is to cover the tip itself, cover the solution following the problem(s) and certainly cover any hand diagram within the solution. The tip itself or the complete hand diagram may often give away the solution to the problem. No one at the table gives you such a head start. Since your aim is improvement, start by considering the problem only. If the tip contains more than one problem, decide on an answer for each of them.

After you have your answers, go back and read the tip. Decide whether any of your answers would now change. Then and only then read the solution and study the hand diagrams involved.

Some of the tips in the bidding section would require you to change your present methods. That is of course up to you, but the tips do encompass methods that are popular among the top players.

On any play or defence problem, your objective is to make your contract as declarer or defeat their contract when defending. Overtricks or extra undertricks are not required unless so stated in the problem. You may assume the setting is teams or rubber bridge.

Do not despair if you fail to find all the right answers. The players who faced the problems at the table also did not come up with the winning move every time. Quite the contrary. Many of the tips and problems were conceived because of the failure at the table.

I will be delighted and satisfied if you are able to apply even a few of the tips. I am sure that if you do, your results will surpass those to date and your game will more frequently reflect *Happy Bridging*.

Ron Klinger
1996

Tip 1 : When cue-bidding below game, you can save space and solve many problems by showing first or second round controls with the first set of cue bids. You can still check on aces / key cards with 4NT.

In standard cue-bidding, kings and singletons are not shown on the first round of cues. This can take the bidding too high to solve the problems.

WEST	W	E	EAST
♠ A Q 7 6	1◇	1♠	♠ K J 10 5 3
♡ 4	3♠	?	♡ A K J
◇ A K 9 6 2			◇ Q 4
♣ Q 9 4			♣ 8 7 2

After the jump-raise, East is worth a slam move but the club layout makes it risky to push these two hands beyond 4♠. If East bids 4♡ to show the ace and may yet have second round control in clubs, West may feel compelled to proceed with 5◇. Now the partnership could be too high.

Showing first or second round controls at once (multi-cues), East's 4♡ not only shows control in hearts but simultaneously denies first and second round control in each minor. West has no problem signing off in 4♠ as the club suit must be wide open. Now, suppose the hands were :

WEST	W	E	EAST
♠ A Q 7 6	1◇	1♠	♠ K J 10 5 3
♡ Q 9 4	3♠	4♡	♡ A K J
◇ A K 9 6 2	?		◇ Q 4
♣ 4			♣ 8 7 2

This time West with control in both minors should continue with 4NT (preferably Roman Key Card Blackwood) and reach the excellent 6♠.

WEST	W	E	EAST
♠ K Q 7 6	2♣	2◇	♠ A 10 9 5 3
♡ A K Q 8 3	2♡	2♠	♡ 7 6
◇ A K	3♠	4♣	◇ 9 8 7 5 3
♣ Q 8	4NT	5◇	♣ 6
	6♠	No	

With 4♣ showing the club control, West has an easy route to 6♠.

Tip 2 : The 6-4 brings in more.

Upgrade your hand if a 6-4 trump fit exists. Upgrade your hand if you have a 6-4 pattern. Be even more optimistic if you have both the 6-4 pattern and a 6-4 trump fit.

Basic point count rarely does justice to the playing strength when a 6-4 trump fit exists. A sensible approach is to add one trick, 3 points, to the value of your hand in addition to the rest of the point count.

Suppose the bidding has started :

WEST	EAST	What action should East take with each of
1♣	1♡	these hands?
3♡	?	

(1)	♠ A 7	(2)	♠ A K 3	(3)	♠ A 3 2
	♡ J 7 6 5 3 2		♡ K 7 6 5 3 2		♡ K 7 6 5 3 2
	◊ 9 8 3		◊ 8		◊ K 9
	♣ 4 2		♣ 9 6 2		♣ K 2

(1) West's jump-raise is not forcing and with a minimum, responder is entitled to pass. With only one obvious winner and 7 points (one for each doubleton), East might be forgiven for considering the hand a minimum. Give yourself 3 more points for the 6-4 fit and East has an easy raise to game. Suppose that partner holds a hand something like —
♠96 ♡A984 ◊A7 ♣AQJ73 and game has respectable chances.

(2) With only 13 points (3 for the singleton), some Easts would settle for game. Add the 3 for the 6-4 fit, making it 16 and slam prospects are clear opposite the expected 16 or so for opener's jump-raise. A cue-bid of 3♠ is a good way to start the slam investigation. Opposite the same opener as in (1), you should be delighted to reach 6♡.

(3) With 15 total points East might be wary of anything more than a small slam, yet opposite the same opener, 7♡ and 7NT have excellent chances.

It follows that if partner opens with a weak 2♡ or 2♠ (6-suit, 6-10 HCP), responder should be eager to bid game with 4-card support even with the slightest values. If game happens to fail, it figures to be a cheap save.

The 6-4 hand pattern plays exceptionally well if a trump fit exists and also tends to produce more tricks than point count would suggest. Take a look at these hands :

WEST	EAST
♠ K Q 5 3	♠ A J 6 2
♡ 8 7	♡ J 6 3
◊ A K 8 5 3 2	◊ 7 4
♣ 7	♣ 9 8 6 2

East-West belong in 4♠ but after 1◊ : 1♠, if West does not push all the way, it is hard to see East accepting any invitation. If spades and diamonds are both 3-2, 4♠ is easy and if either suit breaks 4-1, North-South can make 4♡, so that failing in 4♠ should not prove expensive.

What should West rebid after 1◊ : 1♠? Certainly a jump to 4♠ would solve this problem and some might consider a splinter of 4♣. Regular partnerships could do worse than to harness the jump-rebid in opener's minor, 1◊ : 1♠, 4◊, to describe this hand type.

The jump rebid to four in opener's minor is not needed in a natural sense. Some use it to show a solid minor, A-K-Q-x-x-x or better, plus good support, but you can wait a long time for that to crop up. It should be enough if it shows the 6-4 pattern with four of the six top honours in the two long suits.

Given the power of the 6-4, be wary about opening a weak two with this pattern. With ♠A109754 ♡6 ◊KQ93 ♣82, a 6-loser hand despite the meagre point count, a 1♠ opening is more attractive than 2♠.

With both a 6-4 pattern *and* a 6-4 trump fit, the sky's the limit.

WEST	W	E	EAST
♠ A J 7 6 2	1♠	2♣	♠ K 5
♡ 4	4♣	4◊	♡ A 7 5 2
◊ A Q 3	4♡	4NT	◊ 6
♣ A J 4 2	5♠	7♣	♣ K Q 8 6 5 3

4◊ and 4♡ showed first *or* second-round controls (see Tip 1). With a 6-4 pattern and knowing of the 6-4 trump fit, East was now prepared to bid the grand slam if West held three aces. 7♣ should be an easy make.

Tip 3 : If your long suit has a Suit Quality of 10, be prepared to insist on your suit being trumps.

Suppose the bidding has started :

WEST	EAST	
1♣	1♠	What action should East take with each of
2♣	?	these hands?

(1) ♠ K Q J 10 7 3	(2) ♠ K Q 7 6 4 3	(3) ♠ A Q J 10 7 2
♡ K 7	♡ K 7	♡ K 7 6
◇ 9 8 3	◇ J 8 3	◇ A Q
♣ A 2	♣ A 2	♣ 8 2

The Suit Quality (SQ) test was devised to test the soundness of overcalls, as less than expert players can be prone to overcalling on poor suits. To calculate SQ, count the number of cards in your long suit (Length) and add the number of honour cards in that suit (Strength). The answer is the Suit Quality of that particular suit. For an overcall, the Suit Quality should not be less than the number of tricks for which you are bidding. For example :

♠ J 10 3	The dealer on your right opens with 1♣.
♡ K Q 8 5 3	What action would you take?
◇ 9 8 3	What would your answer be if the opening
♣ A J	bid had been 1♠?

You have five hearts including two honours. Length 5 + Strength 2 = 7. The heart suit is therefore good enough to bid for seven tricks. Over 1♣, you should overcall 1♡. Over 1♠, you would need to call 2♡ but your SQ is 7, not enough for an eight trick contract, and you should pass.

It is true that with a stronger hand you might risk 2♡ but when the decision is borderline, the SQ Test can stop you from foolhardy bids. With significant outside strength, you might reduce the SQ requirement by one but when suit quality is an ingredient of your action, do not dilute the SQ any further.

When assessing SQ, the jack and ten should be counted only when they are accompanied by a higher honour. Thus, A-J-10-x-x is counted as SQ of 8, Q-J-x-x-x as 7, but J-x-x-x-x should be taken as only 5.

The SQ Test also proves useful for weak twos (SQ of 8 needed), so that a suit of Q-10-8-5-3-2 is just good enough while Q-8-6-5-3-2 is not. Likewise, a pre-emptive opening of three should have a suit with SQ 9, while a four-level pre-empt ought to have SQ of 10.

SQ of 10 is significant as it indicates your suit is self-sufficient. Each of these has SQ of 10 : K-Q-J-10-x-x or A-K-J-10-x-x or A-Q-J-x-x-x-x or K-Q-x-x-x-x-x-x. Such suits should play comfortably for no more than one loser if partner has a singleton or better. Even if partner is void in your suit, there is still some chance that you will not lose more than one trick.

With such a powerful suit, you should normally insist on making that suit trumps, especially if it is a major. With a suit of lesser quality, you will need some support from partner. That brings us to the problems opposite.

(1) Partner has shown a minimum opening. You have enough for game and your spades have a SQ of 10. You should bid 4♠ without more ado.

(2) You again have enough for game but your spades are not adequate without assistance from partner. Imagine trying to cope in 4♠ if partner happens to be void in spades. Nothing in the bidding so far has indicated any spades with partner and you need to be more conservative. The jump to 3♠ is forcing, shows a 6-card suit and asks for support with a doubleton.

(3) Again your spades have SQ of 10 but you are too strong to settle for 4♠ when a slam is in the offing. In such a case, continue with a jump to 3♠, forcing. If partner raises to 4♠, you can venture 4NT. If partner bids 3NT, showing a singleton or void in spades, persist with 4♠. Since you are insisting on spades opposite possibly nil support, your spades must be excellent. Hopes for a slam explain why you did not jump straight to 4♠ over 2♣. With very strong clubs and the ace of hearts, partner has enough to move towards slam, but should pass 4♠ with lesser holdings.

Knowing you have an excellent suit can enable partner to bid to slam.

WEST	W	E	EAST
♠ A 5 3	1♣	1♡	♠ J 10 4
♡ Q	2◊	4♡	♡ A K J 8 7 3 2
◊ A K 7 3	6♡	No	◊ 6 2
♣ A K 9 4 2			♣ 3

The ♡Q has huge value after East's jump to 4♡ shows SQ of 10.

Tip 4 : If you have a 6-5 pattern with a 6-card minor and a 5-card major, it will usually work best to start with your 6-card suit.

With a freakish two-suiter, it pays to describe the length of your suits accurately to partner in order to end in the better trump suit. Even when the 5-carder is strong, you should beware of bidding your suits in false order.

Consider this deal from a teams match :

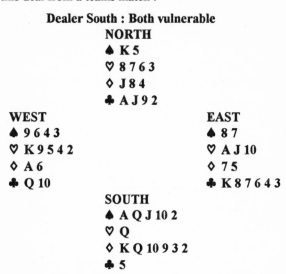

Dealer South : Both vulnerable

NORTH
♠ K 5
♡ 8 7 6 3
◊ J 8 4
♣ A J 9 2

WEST
♠ 9 6 4 3
♡ K 9 5 4 2
◊ A 6
♣ Q 10

EAST
♠ 8 7
♡ A J 10
◊ 7 5
♣ K 8 7 6 4 3

SOUTH
♠ A Q J 10 2
♡ Q
◊ K Q 10 9 3 2
♣ 5

At one table the bidding went :

WEST	NORTH	EAST	SOUTH
			1♠
No	1NT	No	3◊
No	3♠	No	4♠ End

Following the sensible adage 'Trump Length, Lead Length'*, West started with a low heart. East won and returned a heart, ruffed. Down to four trumps, South could not afford to draw all the trumps and then lose the lead to the ace of diamonds. He tried playing diamonds first, but West took the ace and led the king of hearts, eroding South's trumps even further.

South ruffed and played trumps, hoping for a 3-3 break. With the normal 4-2 split, the contract went three down.

*See Tip 46 in *100 Winning Bridge Tips*

At the other table, South described his shape more precisely :

WEST	NORTH	EAST	SOUTH
			1◊
No	1NT	No	4♠
No	5◊	All pass	

This contract proved to be child's play. Declarer drew trumps and lost just to the two red aces.

One way to show a 6-minor, 5-major pattern is South's method above : open with the minor suit and jump to game in the major on the next round. Jumping to game in a new suit promises five cards in that suit. As South opened in a lower-ranking suit, the first suit must be longer (since with two five-card suits, starting with the higher-ranking suit is best). North did well to give preference back to diamonds, choosing the partnership's longer combined trump suit. Even with 3-3 in spades and diamonds, the preference to diamonds is correct since a 4-1 break in the 5-3 fit is not far-fetched and could prove fatal.

With suits of lesser quality, prefer to start with your 6-card suit and then bid your 5-card suit at the cheapest level, followed by a repeat of the 5-card suit at the cheapest level. This sequence is not forcing and could allow you to bail out at a low level.

WEST	W	E	EAST
♠ A 9 7 6 3	1◊	1♡	♠ J 10 2
♡ Q	1♠	1NT	♡ K 8 7 3 2
◊ Q 10 7 5 3 2	2♠	No	◊ 6 4
♣ A			♣ Q J 7

1♠ followed by 2♠ shows five spades and therefore at least six diamonds. East can tell that the honours in hearts and clubs are almost useless and has no ambition to push any further.

There is a school of thought that with 5 spades and 5 clubs, one should open 1♣ and show the spade length later. It pays to be a drop-out from that school as this approach has two drawbacks. Firstly, it may be awkward to convince partner you hold *five* spades if the auction becomes competitive. Secondly, if you do show five spades, partner will not know whether you hold six or more clubs or only five. With 5-5 in the blacks, prefer to start 1♠ and use auctions such as 1♣ : 1♡, 1♠ : 1NT, 2♠ to show the 6-5 patterns.

Tip 5 : If you play transfers after partner's 2NT opening, it is worth creating a structure which allows opener to show a super-fit.

♠ K Q 6 4
♥ A K 3
◊ A 6 2
♣ A J 3

You open 2NT and partner responds 3♥, a transfer to spades. What action would you take?

Suppose you bid 3♠ and partner continues with 3NT. What now?

As partner's transfer may be made on a very, very weak hand, it is not safe for you to bid beyond 3♠ which partner may be intending to pass. Still, it is worth jeopardising the part score in order to increase the chance of locating the best game contract.

If you do bid 3♠ and partner rebids 3NT, you cannot be sure whether 3NT is best or whether 4♠ is the superior spot. Suppose the hands are :

WEST	EAST
♠ K Q 6 4	♠ A 9 7 5 3
♥ A K 3	♥ 8 2
◊ A 6 2	◊ 9 5 4
♣ A J 3	♣ 8 6 2

Despite the 9-card spade fit, 3NT is highly likely to succeed and 4♠ will fail most of the time. The same applies to this layout :

WEST	EAST
♠ K Q 6 4	♠ J 9 7 5 3 2
♥ A K 3	♥ 8 2
◊ A 6 2	◊ 9 5 4
♣ A J 3	♣ 8 6

4♠ has little chance. 3NT is cold on a heart lead and will make most of the time on a diamond or a club lead. It would be normal for East to transfer to spades and pass if West rebids 3♠. That would avoid the poor game in spades but miss the good game in no-trumps.

This method has much to recommend it after a 2NT opening and a transfer to a major :

(a) Transfer to hearts

WEST	EAST
2NT	3◊
?	

(b) Transfer to spades

WEST	EAST
2NT	3♡
?	

Opener rebids as follows :

3NT = 3 or 4 card support for responder's major including two of the top three honours plus instant winners in the outside suits. Instant winners are aces and A-K combinations. The 3NT bid suggests that there will be nine winners opposite Q-x-x-x-x or better or opposite six rags. On both the hands on the opposite page, West would rebid 3NT over 3♡ and East should pass in each case.

Other bids beyond responder's major and excluding 3NT are :

Step 1 (a) 3♠ (b) 4♣ : Super-fit with three key cards

Step 2 (a) 4♣ (b) 4◊ : Super-fit with four key cards

Step 3 (a) 4◊ (b) 4♡ : Super-fit with five key cards

Step 4 (jump raise of responder's suit)(a) 4♡ (b) 4♠ : Super-fit with five trumps but only two key cards

'Super-fit' promises 4-5 trumps and a doubleton outside. With support for responder below super-fit values, simply bid the major, 3♡ in (a) and 3♠ in (b). If opener has super-fit values but also the instant winner requirements for 3NT, prefer the 3NT rebid except when holding all five key cards. If responder has slam ambitions after a super-fit reply, 4NT asks for the queen of trumps and other suit bids can be used as asking bids.

WEST	W	E	EAST
♠ A K 7 6	2NT	3♡	♠ J 10 8 5 3 2
♡ A J	4♡	7♠	♡ 3
◊ A 5 2	No		◊ K Q 8 4 3
♣ A J 8 4			♣ 7

4♡ showed 4-5 spades and all five key cards, allowing East to bid the excellent grand slam at once. Even with ◊ Q-J-8-4-3, East would know that the small slam in spades would be a good bet and could explore the grand slam with an asking bid in diamonds in case West had ◊K as well.

Tip 6 : Where it is clear that no trump suit has been agreed, a jump to 5NT or a no-trumps raise to 5NT is forcing and says 'Partner, pick a slam.'

In many situations, it may be clear to one partner that the values for slam are present but not which is the right slam. In such cases the jump to 5NT shows the values and asks partner to suggest the best slam.

In reply to 5NT, partner should bid a decent 5-card suit that has not been previously shown or a very powerful 5-card suit if that suit has been shown earlier. A very strong 4-card suit (K-Q-J-x or better) can also be shown. With none of these, choose 6NT.

WEST	W	E	EAST
♠ A Q 4	2NT	3♣	♠ K J 10 7
♡ A K 2	3♢	5NT	♡ J 8
♢ K Q J 10	6♢	No	♢ A 6 3
♣ Q 9 5			♣ K 8 7 2

East tried for a spade fit via Stayman and when that failed, East showed slam values with 5NT. With a ruffing value in hearts, East was happy to pass 6♢, as West would have five diamonds or at worst, K-Q-J-x. With weaker diamonds West would have chosen 6NT. As you can see, 6♢ is a much better prospect than 6NT.

The same approach can be taken after a quantitative raise to 4NT. Suppose on the above hand East lacked the ♡J. With only 11 points East might try 4NT over West's 3♢. With a minimum, West would pass but with better values, West would accept the slam invitation. When accepting, a 5-level suit bid should be a powerful 4-card suit or a good 5-card suit and a jump to 6-suit should be a very strong 5-card suit.

Even when a fit is found, 5NT may locate the better slam.

WEST	W	E	EAST
♠ A 9 7 2	2NT	3♣	♠ 10 6 5 4
♡ A J	3♠	5NT	♡ K Q 5 2
♢ K Q 4	6NT	No	♢ A J
♣ A K 6 3			♣ Q J 5

5NT makes no sense here as the Grand Slam Force. East chooses 5NT as West will bid 6♠ with powerful spades and the better 6NT otherwise.

If the partnership agrees that the 5NT Trump Ask (also known as the Grand Slam Force) can be used only after explicit suit agreement, then the scope for the 5NT slam probe ('pick a slam') can be extended. Here is an example after a 12-14 1NT and a transfer to spades :

WEST	W	E	EAST
♠ A 4	1NT	2♥	♠ K 10 7 3 2
♥ Q 8 2	2♠	5NT	♥ K 3
◊ J 10 3	6♣	No	◊ A K Q
♣ K Q 10 7 6			♣ A J 5

Without relays, it is not easy to locate a 5-card minor with the 1NT opener. The 5NT slam probe allows natural bidders to catch up and reach the best slam.

The 5NT probe can also be suitable after fourth-suit forcing :

WEST	W	E	EAST
♠ 9 7	1◊	1♥	♠ A J 3 2
♥ A 2	2♣	2♠	♥ K 10 8 5 3
◊ K Q J 10 3	3♠	5NT	◊ A 6
♣ A Q 5 2	6◊	No	♣ K 4

West's 2♣ denied four spades and so the 3♠ reply to fourth-suit forcing said, 'I have no 3-card heart support, no spade stopper, no 5-5 pattern but I have a strong hand.' (3◊ would show a similar opening but with minimum values.) East trots out 5NT and West's 6◊ shows an excellent 5-card suit, allowing East to pass West in the best contract.

In the 1995 Politiken World Pairs (Denmark), Fred Gitelman and George Mittelman of Canada gained 11 Imps by reaching the best slam via a logical corollary to the 5NT slam probe on these cards :

WEST	W	E	EAST
♠ K 10	1NT	2♣	♠ A J
♥ K 2	2◊	4NT	♥ A J 7 3
◊ A 10 8 3 2	5NT	6◊	◊ Q J 6 4
♣ A J 8 5	No		♣ K 9 2

1NT = 15-17; 2♣ = Stayman; 2◊ = no major; 4NT = slam invitational; 5NT = 'I am accepting the invitation, choose a minor suit if you can.' The diamond finesse was on but the heart and club finesses were not.

Tip 7 : **In a constructive auction, a weak responding hand, one that is below 10 HCP, should use 4NT to suggest slam values (rather than as Blackwood) if responder is unable to make a suitable cue-bid.**

Suppose the bidding has started :

WEST	EAST	What action should East take with each of
2♣	2NT	these hands?
3♥	?	

(1) ♠ Q 7 3	(2) ♠ K Q J 6	(3) ♠ K Q 6 3
♥ K 7 3	♥ 5 2	♥ 5 2
◇ A J 8 3	◇ 10 7 6 2	◇ Q 10 6 2
♣ 10 8 2	♣ K 8 2	♣ K J 9

The 2NT response shows a balanced positive reply with 8+ points. Opener's 3♣ rebid is best played as Stayman and any other suit shows a 5+ suit and asks for 3-card or better support. With long clubs, opener can jump to 4♣ with a 6+ suit and bid 3♣ followed by 4♣ with five clubs.

West's 3♥ above shows 5+ hearts. With 3-4 hearts, responder shows the support with a cue-bid if possible. East #1 therefore bids 4◇, showing the diamond control and heart support. If playing multi-cues (see Tip #1), East's 4◇ simultaneously denies first or second control in either black suit, quite a lot of information from just one cue.

East #2 bids 3NT to deny heart support and also to show a minimum 2NT response (8-9 points or an especially robust 7). Over that, opener can pass or explore further.

East #3 lacks support for hearts but is too strong to risk 3NT being passed out. The bid is 4NT which carries the message : 'I have only two hearts but slam is still on the agenda as I have 10+ points.' Over 4NT, opener can bid a decent second suit or use the 5NT slam probe (see Tip #6). Over 5NT, responder would introduce a powerful 4-card suit or could show Q-x or stronger doubleton support for opener's original suit. On the actual hand, responder #3 would bid 6NT over 5NT.

WEST	EAST	What action should East #2 above take if
2♣	2NT	West rebids 4♣ (4+ suit) over East's 3NT rebid?
3♥	3NT	
4♣	?	

At this point a bid of 4◊ or 4♠ should be taken as a cue bid with support for clubs. 5♣ would show support without first or second round control in either diamonds or spades (no cue available). What should responder do without support for clubs? There are two actions, one showing poor values and one suggesting slam prospects.

WEST	W	E	EAST
♠ A	2♣	2NT	♠ K Q J 6
♡ A K Q J 6	3♡	3NT	♡ 5 2
◊ K 4 3	4♣	4NT	◊ 10 7 6 2
♣ A Q 7 3	6♡	No	♣ K 8 2

Over 4♣, without club support and a poor hand within the range expected for the 3NT rebid, East should bid 4♡. As 3-card heart support has already been denied, 4♡ would be an attempt to sign off with a wholly unsuitable hand, one with excess jacks perhaps, something like :

$$♠ K J 5 3 \quad ♡ 5 2 \quad ◊ Q J 5 2 \quad ♣ J 8 4$$

The actual East is worth 4NT, a stronger action than 4♡. 4NT suggests the hand is still suitable for slam within the confines previously described. 9 HCP is maximum, the spades provide a source of tricks and the king of clubs is bound to be useful on the bidding. With solid hearts, West sensibly choose 6♡ just in case the ◊K needs to be protected on lead.

WEST	EAST #1	EAST #2
♠ K Q J 9 2	♠ 4	♠ 4
♡ A K Q	♡ 7 6 5 2	♡ 6 5 2
◊ A 10 4 3	◊ K Q 9 6 2	◊ J 9 8 7 6 2
♣ A	♣ Q 5 3	♣ 8 4 2

WEST	EAST
2♣	2◊
2♠	3◊
4◊	?

East #1, just short of a positive reply, has excellent values for slam but no convenient cue-bid. East #1 bids 4NT to show the slam prospects and West should jump to 6◊. East #2 has no discernible slam values and should simply raise to 5◊ which West should pass.

Tip 8 : **After a single raise in a minor suit, a change of suit by opener is strong and forcing, usually an unbalanced hand pattern. With values too strong to sign off, responder can bid a suit in which length has previously been denied in order to show one or more high cards in that suit.**

After 1♣ : 2♣ or 1◊ : 2◊, it is a long way to the minor suit game and slam prospects are even more remote. Yet, if responder's values are in the right place and the partnership can locate them, nothing is impossible. How do you think the following hands should be bid?

WEST	EAST
♠ A Q 7 5	♠ K 8 3
♡ A K 3 2	♡ Q 7
◊ 6	◊ 9 5 4
♣ A Q 8 2	♣ K 9 6 4 3

An expert pair might produce this auction and there is no reason why you and your partner cannot do the same.

WEST	EAST
1♣	2♣
2♡	2♠
3♠	4NT
6♣	No

2♡ showed values in hearts and was forcing. Having denied four cards in either major, East now bid 2♠ to show at least one top card there. West's 3♠, still forcing, completed the hand pattern and indicated short diamonds. By highlighting the short suit, West is asking East to demote values in diamonds.

East's 4NT, a jump for joy (see Tip #7), indicates an ideal hand, all the values in the right place if West has slam ambitions. Typically this jump to 4NT would show three useful cards with responder. West needs no more urging and bids the small slam.

If West happened to be looking at this collection :

♠ A Q 7 5　　♡ A K 3 2　　◊ - - -　　♣ A Q 8 7 2

East's 4NT would enable West to jump to 7♣.

With a dreadful collection, East would sign off in 3♣ over 2♡ on a hand such as this :

♠ 8 4 3   ♡ 7 5   ◊ Q 5 2   ♣ K J 6 4 3

With strength in both unbid suits, East should jump to 3NT over 2♡ with something like this :

♠ K J 3   ♡ 7 5   ◊ K Q 10   ♣ 9 6 5 4 3

Here is another example :

WEST	W	E	EAST
♠ A J 10	1◊	2◊	♠ 7 4
♡ 6	2♠	3♣	♡ 10 5 2
◊ A Q 9 7 2	4♣	5◊	◊ K J 8 3
♣ K Q 7 3	No		♣ A 9 5 2

Just as responder can show high cards in a suit already denied, so opener can show strength in a suit denied by responder. That makes 2♠ a safe action by West after the raise to 2◊. East's 3♣ shows a top card there and West's 4♣ completes the picture. East's jump to 5◊ shows two useful cards (4NT would show three good cards) and that is enough for these combined hands. A raise to 5♣ instead of 5◊ would suggest a 2-2-4-5 and enable West to raise to 6♣, playing East for ◊K and ♣A.

When opener makes a new suit rebid after the minor suit raise, a suit by-passed is often the weak point of the hand. In the auction above, 2♠ suggests that hearts could be a problem and the 2♡ rebid in the auction on page 22 means diamonds might be a worry. If responder bids the problem suit, this shows one stopper there and suggests 3NT might be best if opener does have something useful there.

WEST	W	E	EAST
♠ A J 10	1◊	2◊	♠ 7 4
♡ K	2♠	3♡	♡ A 10 2
◊ A Q 9 7 2	3NT	No	◊ K J 8 3
♣ K 10 7 3			♣ 9 6 5 2

3♡ shows a respectable raise and one stopper in hearts. West judges that the singleton king is just the bolster needed for 3NT.

Tip 9 : A splinter bid is an extremely useful way to show trump support for partner and a short suit at the same time. A weak responder after a 2♣ opening should be eager to use a splinter as the knowledge of the support and shortage may be just what opener needs to judge slam prospects.

A double jump bid in a new suit by responder is commonly played these days as a 'splinter'. These would be splinter sequences :

(1) WEST	EAST	(2) WEST	EAST	(3) WEST	EAST
1♥	3♠	1♥	4♣	1♠	4♦

Responder is showing 4+ trumps, a singleton or void in the suit bid and enough high card values for game, usually 11+ HCP. Since the trump support and high card values are roughly enough for game, the splinter is a short suit try for slam. The message to opener is that if the short suit can generate at least two useful ruffs, slam is likely. Even with a minimum opening, a holding such as x-x-x or A-x-x opposite the short suit should light up opener's eyes.

Opener can also make a splinter rebid. If responder has bid a major at the one-level, the same double jumps in a new suit would be splinters. After a two-level response, any change of suit is forcing so that a jump in a new suit can be played as a splinter. These are splinters by opener :

(4) WEST	EAST	(5) WEST	EAST	(6) WEST	EAST
1♥	1♠	1♥	2♦	1♠	2♥
4♦		4♣		4♦	

As opener's reverse is forcing for one round, the jump-shift into a reverse suit is commonly played as a splinter. West's rebids here are splinters :

(7) WEST	EAST	(8) WEST	EAST	(9) WEST	EAST
1♦	2♣	1♦	1NT	1♣	2♣
3♥		3♠		3♠	

In (7) 2♥ would be forcing. 3♥ shows 4+ club support and shortage in hearts. In (8), 2♠ would be forcing for one round. The jump to 3♠ shows short spades and 6+ diamonds in a hand too strong for a 3♦ rebid, perhaps 17-18 points with seven diamonds. After suit agreement, a change of suit would be forcing and strong (see Tip #8) and so the jump bid after suit agreement is a splinter with extra length in the suit opened.

If you use transfers after a 1NT opening, a transfer followed by a jump in a new suit shows a 6+ suit, shortage in the suit bid and slam prospects.

WEST	W	E	EAST
♠ A K J	1NT	2♡	♠ 10 9 8 7 5 3 2
♡ K 8 7 2	2♠	4◊	♡ A 9 6
◊ 4 2	6♠	No	◊ 10
♣ K 10 8 5			♣ A Q

2♡ = transfer, 4◊ = splinter. In the 1995 Australian Open Pairs, two internationals, Alan Walsh, West, and George Havas produced this sequence to reach the superb 24-point slam, found by only one other pair.

Splinters are particularly useful for a weak responder to a 2♣ opening. Often the responder may hold little useful outside of support and a short suit. The splinter enables responder to show such values.

WEST	W	E	EAST
♠ A Q 7	2♣	2◊	♠ K 6 3
♡ A K Q 8 7 2	2♡	4♣	♡ 9 5 4 3
◊ A	4◊	4♠	◊ 8 7 6 3 2
♣ A 4 2	7♡		♣ 5

4♣ = short clubs with heart support, 4◊ = cue-bid, 4♠ = cue-bid (first or second round control — see Tip #1) and West's euphoria is unbounded.

Under normal circumstances a splinter should include 4+ trumps. The reason is that the opponents may lead a trump and if partner has to lose the lead in your singleton suit, a second trump lead reduces dummy's ruffing potential to one trick. Nevertheless, it is reasonable to splinter with just three trumps opposite a 2♣ opener since it is quite likely that opener has the ace opposite your singleton.

WEST	W	E	EAST
♠ A K J 8 7 5 2	2♣	2◊	♠ Q 9 4
♡ A 7 2	2♠	4♡	♡ 6
◊ A K Q	7♠	No	◊ 9 5 4 3
♣ - - -			♣ 8 7 6 5 2

Given the 2◊ negative and that 3♡ would be forcing, it is sensible to play 4♡ as a splinter. That makes West's rebid simple. Had East bid 4◊, West would try 6♠, hoping for East's red suit holdings to be reversed.

Tip 10 : If you have no other convenient action, it is reasonable to splinter in a suit where you hold king-doubleton.

Traditionally, a splinter bid shows a singleton or a void and therefore partner can see losers in that suit eliminated by ruffing. King-doubleton can perform the same function in some situations. If partner has A-x-x, then K-x opposite is as good as a singleton, probably even better. Partner would picture no loser there and would not be misled. Likewise with Q-x-x partner would expect one loser in the suit and the K-x holding will not let partner down.

It may not always be so rosy. With J-x-x or worse in the suit, partner would count on only one loser and with K-x in dummy, there is a 50% chance of there being two losers. Why be gloomy? Think positive : you have a 50% chance of losing only one trick. Finesses favour the bold.

Here are two examples where responder did decide to splinter on a K-x holding without ill effects :

WEST	W	E	EAST
♠ A	2♣	2♠	♠ K 9 5 4 3
♡ A 6 3 2	3♢	4♡	♡ K 7
♢ A K 10 9 6 2	7♢	No	♢ Q 5 4 3
♣ A K			♣ J 7

The jump to 4♡ was a splinter agreeing diamonds. That made it easy for West to envisage no losers. West might have checked for the trump queen to make doubly sure of the grand slam but the key to success was the 4♡ splinter. Had East just raised to 4♢, West would not have been able to diagnose the grand slam for East might then have held :

♠ K 9 5 4 3   ♡ K 7 5   ♢ Q 5 4   ♣ J 7

In that case the grand slam would have been much less attractive.

WEST	W	E	EAST
♠ A K Q 4 3	1♠	2♣	♠ 5 2
♡ A J 9 3 2	2♡	4♢	♡ K Q 8 7
♢ A 8 2	5NT	6♢	♢ K 3
♣ - - -	7♡	No	♣ K Q J 8 5

4♢ = splinter agreeing hearts. 5NT = Trump Ask. 6♢ = two top trumps.

Tips 11-20   COMPETITIVE BIDDING

Tip 11 : Do not raise partner's suit if you are strong in the enemy suit and would prefer to defend than to sacrifice.

With length in partner's overcall suit, it is attractive to show your support. It is wise to temper this desire when you are also strong in the suit bid by the opposition. Raising partner may tempt an ill-timed sacrifice. That is precisely what occurred on this deal from a national championship :

Dealer West : Nil vulnerable

```
                    NORTH
                    ♠ 7 6 2
                    ♡ Q 10 8 5
                    ◊ J 7 3 2
                    ♣ A 10
   WEST                              EAST
   ♠ A J 5 3                         ♠ 10 8 4
   ♡ K J 9 7                         ♡ A 6 4 3
   ◊ - - -                           ◊ Q 6 4
   ♣ K 9 8 3 2                       ♣ Q J 5
                    SOUTH
                    ♠ K Q 9
                    ♡ 2
                    ◊ A K 10 9 8 5
                    ♣ 7 6 4
```

WEST	NORTH	EAST	SOUTH
1♣	No	1♡	2◊
3♡	4◊	4♡	5◊
No	No	Double	All pass

A heart was led followed by a spade shift. In the fullness of time, South lost two spades, a heart and a club for down two. This was not a sound investment as 4♡ was fated to go at least one down.

South might have left the decision to North but the 4◊ raise meant few defensive tricks could be expected from diamonds and the save seemed cheap. With such strong hearts, North should pass 3♡ and choose to defend.

Tip 12 : With a 6-minor, 5-major pattern as an overcaller, you will usually be better placed to find your right spot by bidding the 6-card suit first. With reasonable suits, you can afford to bid game in your major suit on the next round.

Neither South followed this advice on the following deal from the 1994 European Junior Championships, won by Great Britain.

Dealer East : Both vulnerable

NORTH
♠ K 7
♡ 8 6
◊ A 8 6 4
♣ A 10 5 4 2

WEST	EAST
♠ 6 4	♠ A 8 3 2
♡ K Q 7 3 2	♡ A J 10 9 4
◊ J 2	◊ Q
♣ K J 9 3	♣ Q 8 7

SOUTH
♠ Q J 10 9 5
♡ 5
◊ K 10 9 7 5 3
♣ 6

With Great Britain East-West, the bidding went :

WEST	NORTH	EAST	SOUTH
		1♡	1♠
4♡	Double	All pass	

The ♣6 went to North's ace, followed by a club ruff. A spade shift instead of a diamond allowed East to win, draw trumps and make the doubled game.

At the other table, with Great Britain North-South :

WEST	NORTH	EAST	SOUTH
		1♡	1♠
2NT (1)	3♡ (2)	4◊ (3)	4♠
No	No	Double	All pass

(1) Heart raise (2) Strong hand (3) Shortage

West chose a trump lead and South made eleven tricks in sleep. A heart lead would have been more testing. To avoid losing control, declarer needs to discard a diamond on the second heart.

Both North-Souths missed their ten-card fit because neither South produced the best route : overcall 2◊ and if East-West bid 4♡, compete further with 4♠. How neat, convenient and accurate. Even if North has not supported sooner, the preference to 5◊ is obvious and there are no problems in that contract. Note the power here again of the 6-4 fit (see Tip #2). The danger in bidding the spades first and showing the diamonds later is that partner may give you preference to the wrong suit.

With a significantly stronger 6-5, even a 3-loser hand, it is safe enough to start with a simple overcall. It is highly unlikely that the bidding will die at a low level when you hold such a freakish hand.

When the opponents own the spade suit, you may be obliged to compete to the five-level in one of your suits. It is still a short-sighted approach to start with the shorter suit.

♠ 3	The dealer on your right opens with 1♠.
♡ K Q 10 5 3	What action would you take?
◊ A Q J 8 7 2	What would your answer be if the opening
♣ J	bid had been 1♣?

Over 1♠, some would choose 2♡. They reason that the opponents may well reach 4♠ and they can then compete with 5◊, asking partner to choose between the red suits. The flaw is that partner is likely to give preference to hearts when holding equal length in the red suits. That could be fatal if you have to ruff a black suit early and trumps are not friendly.

The better sequence is 2◊ initially, followed by 4NT if they reach 4♠. 4NT in a competitive auction shows a freak two-suiter with your bid suit the longer. It could be 6-7 diamonds with just 4 clubs but if partner does choose 5♣, your removal to 5◊ will show the red suits and greater length in diamonds. Partner can pass 5◊ or choose 5♡. With 3 hearts - 2 diamonds, partner should prefer the 6-2 fit. The 6-card trump suit is more resilient against a 4-1 trump break, which is often the undoing of the 5-3 fit.

If the opening bid is 1♣, you should start with a 1◊ overcall and not 1♡. Bid 4♡ on the next round if available. If the opponents have already reached 4♠, you should compete further as above, with the 4NT two-suiter takeout.

Tip 13 : If partner has made a takeout double, do not pass for penalties with a weak holding in their trump suit.

EAST	Dealer East : North-South vulnerable			
♠ Q 7 4 3	WEST	NORTH	EAST	SOUTH
♡ A J 4			No	2♠ (1)
◊ 10 5 4	Dble	No	?	
♣ 6 5 3	(1) Weak two, decent 6-card suit, 6-10 HCP			

West's double is for takeout. What action should East take playing natural methods? What if East-West play the Lebensohl Convention where a reply of 2NT is artificial (asking the doubler to bid 3♣) and normally the prelude to a weak takeout, while a suit bid at the three level shows respectable values, usually in the 7-11 point range?

To pass partner's takeout double for penalties at the one level requires a stronger trump holding than declarer. The minimum acceptable is a five-card holding no worse than K-Q-J-x-x. Even then you may not score as much in penalties as you might if you declared no-trumps.

If that is the expectancy for a penalty pass at the one-level, how much stronger must you be to pass partner's takeout double after a weak-two opening which shows a respectable 6-card suit? Here even five good trumps may not be enough.

On the problem above, passing 2♠ doubled should not have occurred to East even for a fleeting second. When playing natural methods, a non-forcing 2NT response is the sensible choice. That may not have led to glory on the actual deal, but East cannot bear the blame for that.

The Lebensohl 2NT is useful after the double of a weak two. It enables the advancer to differentiate between the woeful hands (0-6 points) and the respectable hands (7-11 points) with some chance for game.

With a rotten hand, advancer bids 2NT, asking the doubler to bid 3♣. Advancer may then pass 3♣ or attempt to sign off cheaply in another suit. If the doubler is particularly strong, a 4-loser hand is shown by refusing to bid 3♣ and a 3-loser hand bids the enemy suit over 2NT as a force to game.

In the 7-11 range, advancer bids a suit at the three level without going through 2NT. Such a bid is encouraging but not forcing.

If playing Lebensohl, East's best move is to use the 2NT escape route. It is true that East does have 7 points, but the ♠Q is likely to be useless and the lack of a 4-card suit outside spades further downgrades the hand. After West bids 3♣, East should remove to 3♡, likely to be the best combined suit.

At the table East shirked his responsibility and left the double in. Partner started with a top diamond. How would you feel on this layout?

```
                        NORTH
                        ♠ 8 6
                        ♡ Q 7 3 2
                        ◇ 9 2
                        ♣ A K Q 10 9
        WEST                                EAST
        ♠ 9                                 ♠ Q 7 4 3
        ♡ K 10 9 8 6                        ♡ A J 4
        ◇ A K Q J                           ◇ 10 5 4
        ♣ J 7 4                             ♣ 6 5 3
                        SOUTH
                        ♠ A K J 10 5 2
                        ♡ 5
                        ◇ 8 7 6 3
                        ♣ 8 2
```

At trick 2, West shifted to a club and declarer finessed the jack of spades next, followed by another club to dummy. A third club was played, safe even if East had started with just two clubs and the heart loser was discarded. East ruffed the fourth club and was overruffed. South now played a diamond, won perforce by West who could not remove dummy's last trump. South ruffed West's heart exit, ruffed a diamond in dummy and came away with ten tricks. Why suffer all this when 3♡ East-West could be made?

Just deserts, you say, for that awful pass by East? Would that it were so! In real life, dummy had only one trump (and six clubs) and South's spades were A-K-10-9-5-2. West actually had a 2-4-5-2 pattern and did start with a top diamond followed by a club switch. While declarer could have made it (cash two trumps and play on clubs), this was an unlikely line as East figured to have Q-J-x-x-x in trumps. In practice the contract failed by one trick and East would be unlikely to regret his passing fancy (fantasy).

Tip 14 : If you make a penalty double, or pass a takeout double for penalties, when you hold support for partner's suit, you had better be right. Success is the only vindication because most of the time such a decision will be wrong even when you have an excellent holding in the enemy suit.

(1)   **Dealer North : East-West vulnerable**

WEST	NORTH	EAST	SOUTH
	No	2♠ (1)	3♥
?			

(1) 5+ spades and a 5+ minor, 7-11 points

What action should West take with :

♠ K Q 4 2   ♥ K J 9 7 6   ◇ Q 7   ♣ K 9

(2)   **Dealer North : Nil vulnerable**

WEST	NORTH	EAST	SOUTH
	No	2♥ (1)	2♠
?			

(1) 5+ hearts and a 5+ minor, 7-11 points

What action should West take with :

♠ A J 9 6 5 4   ♥ 7 4 2   ◇ Q 3   ♣ A 8

(3)   **Dealer North : Nil vulnerable**

WEST	NORTH	EAST	SOUTH
	No	1♠ (1)	2♠ (2)
Dble (3)	2NT (4)	No	3♣
?			

(1) Playing 5-card majors
(2) Michaels cue-bid, 5+ hearts, 5+ minor, 7-11 points
(3) Angling for penalties
(4) Asking for South's minor suit

What action should West take with :

♠ 9 5 2   ♥ A Q J 9   ◇ A 10 9 7   ♣ A J

The best penalty doubles at a low level occur when you are strong in their suit (4+ trumps and 2+ trump tricks are almost the irreducible minimum), short in partner's suit and your side owns at least half the high card points. Remove any one factor and you are playing with fire.

(1) At the table, West doubled 3♡ for penalties. The complete deal looked like this :

```
                   NORTH
                   ♠ 10 7 6 3
                   ♡ 5 3
                   ◊ K 5 4
                   ♣ A J 6 2
   WEST                               EAST
   ♠ K Q 4 2                          ♠ A J 9 8 5
   ♡ K J 9 7 6                        ♡ - - -
   ◊ Q 7                              ◊ A 8 6 3 2
   ♣ K 9                              ♣ 10 7 5
                   SOUTH
                   ♠ - - -
                   ♡ A Q 10 8 4 2
                   ◊ J 10 9
                   ♣ Q 8 4 3
```

South's 3♡ might look suspect but being void in the enemy suit makes such actions safer than they appear. West led the king of spades and South ruffed. The jack of diamonds was covered by the queen and East captured dummy's king. As the early play marked East already with two aces, South was now confident that West held all the missing trumps to account for the double.

East returned a diamond at trick 3, taken by the 10. A low club went to dummy's jack, followed by a spade ruff. On the next low club, West's king appeared and was topped, followed by another spade ruff. South had won six of the first seven tricks and this was the end-position :

                                    ♠ 10
                                    ♡ 5 3
                                    ◇ 5
                                    ♣ 6 2
        ♠ 4   ♠ A J
        ♡ K J 9 7 6   ♡ - - -
        ◇ - - -   ◇ 8 6 3
        ♣ - - -   ♣ 10
                                    ♠ - - -
                                    ♡ A Q 10
                                    ◇ 9
                                    ♣ Q 8

Clearly West would have done better by supporting East's spades. On a number of lines 4♠ can succeed but no matter what the outcome in 4♠ might be, it would be far preferable to South's making 3♡ doubled.

(2) West could scarcely believe his good fortune with such magnificent trumps and he doubled 2♠ eagerly. Things soon took a turn for the worse.

                            NORTH
                            ♠ 7
                            ♡ Q J 10 3
                            ◇ K 10 9 6
                            ♣ Q J 4 2
        WEST   EAST
        ♠ A J 9 6 5 4   ♠ 3
        ♡ 7 4 2   ♡ A K 8 6 5
        ◇ Q 3   ◇ J 7 5 4 2
        ♣ A 8   ♣ 10 6
                            SOUTH
                            ♠ K Q 10 8 2
                            ♡ 9
                            ◇ A 8
                            ♣ K 9 7 5 3

West led the 4 of hearts to East's king. The 3 of spades switch went to the king and ace and West shifted to the queen of diamonds taken by dummy's king. The queen of hearts was led, covered by the ace and ruffed by declarer with the 2 of spades. After cashing the ace of diamonds, declarer led a low club. West took the ace and exited with a club. This was won in dummy and a club was discarded on the jack of hearts.

After eight tricks declarer had scored five tricks and was left with two clubs and ♠Q-10-8. West had five spades left. Declarer led clubs twice which West had to ruff each time and allow declarer to score his remaining three trumps and make the doubled contract. It would have been cheaper for West to pass or to raise to 3♡.

(3) West decided to double 3♣ for penalties. He believed his strong heart holding would compensate for his meagre trump holding. How wrong!

NORTH
♠ Q 10 7 4
♡ - - -
◊ K J 8 5 4
♣ 10 9 8 2

WEST
♠ 9 5 2
♡ A Q J 9
◊ A 10 9 7
♣ A J

EAST
♠ A K J 8 6 3
♡ 7 5 2
◊ 6 2
♣ Q 7

SOUTH
♠ - - -
♡ K 10 8 6 4 3
◊ Q 3
♣ K 6 5 4 3

West led a spade, ruffed, and South's ◊Q was taken by the ace. South ruffed the next spade and played a diamond to the king, followed by the ◊J. East ruffed with the ♣7 and South overruffed with the king. After a heart ruff, spade ruff, heart ruff, East ruffed the diamond exit from dummy with the ♣Q. The result was 3♣ doubled made while East would have had a comfortable time in 4♠ despite the 4-0 break.

Over 3♣, West might jump to 4♠ or cue-bid 3♡ or 4♣ to show strength.

Tip 15 : A pre-emptive jump to game as an overcall is sometimes made on a better hand than might be expected for a pre-emptive action. If so, the pre-empter is entitled to bid again, despite the general advice that a pre-emptive bidder should bid once and once only.

Dealer West : Both vulnerable

WEST	NORTH	EAST	SOUTH
1♡	No	2♣	4♠
5♣	No	No	?

What action should South take with :

♠ A K Q 10 7 4 2   ♡ 8 5   ◊ K J 6 3   ♣ - - -

With only four losers, South has a very strong playing hand. Give partner as little as the queen of diamonds and 5♠ might be just one down while 5♣ is making easily. On the other hand, partner might have a few defensive cards in hearts and clubs but expecting nothing but spades from South, North might have little reason to double.

In such situations, the partnership might adopt the principle that double by the pre-empter says 'Partner, please do more.' Partner leaves the double in with defensive prospects, otherwise raises partner's suit. This was the layout on the deal which produced the above auction

NORTH
♠ 5 3
♡ Q 10 3
◊ A 10 7 5 4 2
♣ 7 2

WEST
♠ 9
♡ A K J 9 4 2
◊ 8
♣ K 10 9 5 4

EAST
♠ J 8 6
♡ 7 6
◊ Q 9
♣ A Q J 8 6 3

SOUTH
♠ A K Q 10 7 4 2
♡ 8 5
◊ K J 6 3
♣ - - -

Both sides can make eleven tricks and, provided the defence cashes out accurately, no more than eleven tricks. With only one clear defensive trick, North should have no trouble removing South's double to 5♠. Par on the deal is for East-West to save in 6♣ but that would be difficult after this sequence. Note the calamity if South chooses to pass 5♣.

Another common use for double by a pre-empter is lead-directing, indicating a void and a desire to ruff. The double asks partner to try to deduce the void and lead that suit. That use can be suitable for an opening pre-empt but for an overcall pre-empt to game, which tends to be less disciplined than an opening pre-empt, the 'Please-do-more double' has greater frequency. If you choose otherwise, it is still sensible to use this meaning for the double when the pre-empter is on lead.

The double can be harnessed for a pre-emptive jump to game :

Dealer West : Both vulnerable

WEST	NORTH	EAST	SOUTH
1♡	1♠	4♡	4♠
No	No	?	

What action should East take with :

♠ 7 ♡ J 10 8 7 4 3 ◊ 3 ♣ K Q 6 4 2

East has more than the expected playing strength for the jump to game but a unilateral decision to bid 5♡ is not recommended. 'Double', indicating the desire to bid 5♡ but allowing partner the option to pass, is better.

Other pre-emptive actions, such as the unusual 2NT or a Michaels Cue, also lend themselves to the 'Please-do-more-double'.

Dealer North : Both vulnerable

WEST	NORTH	EAST	SOUTH
	1♠	2♠	4♠
No	No	?	

What action should East take with :

♠ - - - ♡ A J 10 7 3 2 ◊ K Q 10 9 5 ♣ 6 5

East is better than expected for the Michaels Cue. The double will indicate the desire to bid on but allow partner to pass with spade values. If in the slightest doubt, partner should not leave the double in.

Tip 16 : In a competitive auction, if you intend to push to the five-level after your side has found a trump fit, you may be sacrificing or issuing a slam invitation. It is important to find a way to distinguish the two.

Dealer West : East-West vulnerable

WEST	NORTH	EAST	SOUTH
1♥	No	3♥ (1)	3♠
4♥	4♠	No	No
?			

(1) Limit raise, 10-12 total points, about 8 losers

What action should West take with :

(A) ♠ 4 ♥ K Q J 9 8 5 ◊ K Q 6 3 2 ♣ Q

(B) ♠ 4 ♥ A K J 9 5 ◊ A K 6 3 ♣ K 7 3

With (A), West has little defence against 4♠ and even at the vulnerability, 5♥ can hardly be expensive. Give partner two aces and 5♥ is highly likely to make. Partner will not have three aces so 6♥ is not in the picture. West should bid 5♥.

With (B), West was content to bid just 4♥ over 3♠ as some of partner's values could have been wasted in spades. When North raised to 4♠ and East did not double, West can envisage that partner's points may well all be in the right place and that 6♥ might be possible.

In order to suggest slam prospects, West should continue with 4NT. As East-West had already settled in game, this should not be interpreted as Blackwood but simply as a slam suggestion based on the bidding so far.

Partner might have either of these hands :

(C) ♠ 8 3 ♥ Q 8 7 2 ◊ Q 5 2 ♣ A Q 10 4

(D) ♠ Q 3 ♥ Q 8 7 2 ◊ 8 5 2 ♣ A Q 10 4

On (C), with nothing wasted in spades and ten working points in high cards, East should accept the invitation and bid 6♥. On (D), there is wastage in spades and East's effective high card content has dropped to eight. Now 5♥ is enough.

Tip 17 : In a competitive auction, if you intend to push to the five-level after your side has found a trump fit and you are not on lead, a new suit bid by you is lead-directing and not slam-suggesting.

Dealer West : East-West vulnerable

WEST	NORTH	EAST	SOUTH
1♠	2♣	3♣ (1)	5♣
?			

(1) Spade support and equal to a limit raise to 3♠ or stronger

What action should West take with each of these hands?

(A) ♠ A 7 6 3 2	(B) ♠ A K 7 6 3	(C) ♠ A Q 7 6 3 2
♡ K J 3	♡ K J 3	♡ 3
◇ K 7	◇ K 4	◇ A K J
♣ Q J 5	♣ 9 5 4	♣ 9 5 4

The opposition bidding plus your club holding indicates that partner is short in clubs and in each case you are strong enough to have reached 4♠ without the interference.

With (A), West should double because of the trick in clubs, the balanced nature of the hand and the lack of anything more than the high card values for game.

With (B), West is entitled to bid 5♠. As the high card values are enough for game, no wastage in clubs gives you a good chance for success at the five-level. Suppose East has these cards :

$$♠ Q 9 8 5 \quad ♡ A Q 4 2 \quad ◇ Q 10 6 3 \quad ♣ 2$$

Opposite West (A), 5♠ would fail and so you must take what you can from 5♣ doubled. Facing West (B), 5♠ is almost a certainty and you are hardly likely to score enough from 5♣ doubled to compensate.

With (C), West should bid 5◇, asking East to bid 5♠ but to lead a diamond if the opponents happen to sacrifice in 6♣. You must not bid 5♠ which could lead to a serious accident. If they bid on to 6♣, doubled, a spade lead by East might hand them the slam if either opponent has a spade void whereas the diamond lead is a much safer start.

Tip 18 : If you have a weak hand overall but exceptional length in partner's suit, try to muddy the waters for the opposition.

(1)   **Dealer West : Nil vulnerable**

WEST	NORTH	EAST	SOUTH
1♠	No	?	

What action should East take with these cards?

♠ A Q J 10 8 5 2   ♡ 9 7   ◇ 3   ♣ 8 6 2

(2)   **Dealer East : Nil vulnerable**

WEST	NORTH	EAST	SOUTH
		2♠ (1)	3♡
3♠	?		

(1) Acol two, 8+ playing tricks with a strong spade suit

What action should North take with these cards?

♠ - - -   ♡ K Q 8 7 6 3   ◇ 10 5   ♣ J 10 7 5 3

Solutions

(1)
```
                    NORTH
                    ♠ - - -
                    ♡ 10 5 3 2
                    ◇ K 9 5 4 2
                    ♣ J 9 7 4
      WEST                          EAST
      ♠ K 9 7 6 4                   ♠ A Q J 10 8 5 2
      ♡ Q 6                         ♡ 9 7
      ◇ A J                         ◇ 3
      ♣ K Q 10 5                    ♣ 8 6 2
                    SOUTH
                    ♠ 3
                    ♡ A K J 8 4
                    ◇ Q 10 8 7 6
                    ♣ A 3
```

There is no 'right' answer for situations like these. As you have a mighty fit in spades, the opponents will have a strong fit elsewhere. One cannot quarrel with the textbook bid of 4♠ since that requires them to start at the five-level. However, one can be creative in such positions without advertising your exceptional support. It does not *always* pay to advertise.

At the table, East responded 2♥ (!) and the bidding went like this :

WEST	NORTH	EAST	SOUTH
1♠	No	2♥	No
2NT	No	4♠	All pass

4♠ made easily while 5♦ is cold for North-South as is 5♥ barring the unlikely start of ace and another diamond. One can hardly blame South for passing over 2♥ but had East jumped to 4♠, South might well have made a takeout bid (double or 4NT). Full marks to East for initiative.

(2)

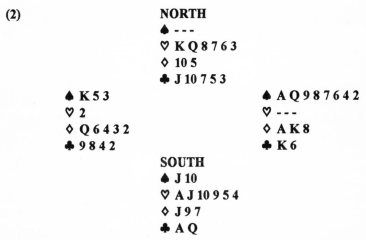

```
                    NORTH
                    ♠ - - -
                    ♥ K Q 8 7 6 3
                    ♦ 10 5
                    ♣ J 10 7 5 3
   ♠ K 5 3                        ♠ A Q 9 8 7 6 4 2
   ♥ 2                            ♥ - - -
   ♦ Q 6 4 3 2                    ♦ A K 8
   ♣ 9 8 4 2                      ♣ K 6
                    SOUTH
                    ♠ J 10
                    ♥ A J 10 9 5 4
                    ♦ J 9 7
                    ♣ A Q
```

With such a huge fit in hearts, North's aim was to buy the contract. This is what happened :

WEST	NORTH	EAST	SOUTH
		2♠	3♥
3♠	4♦!?	4♠	5♦
No	5♥	6♠	No
No	7♥	Double	All pass

6♠ by East is unbeatable but the icing on the cake was the spade lead ruffed, ♥K, club to the queen, ♣A. Making 7♥ doubled.

Tip 19 : If the opponents have shown a strong trump fit and you have 3+ cards in their suit, it is safe to take action on seemingly weak hands.

(1)   **Dealer North : Both vulnerable**

WEST	NORTH	EAST	SOUTH
	1♠	No	No
2♡	No	4♡	?

What should South do with :

♠ - - -   ♡ 9 5 3   ◊ J 10 8 7 6 3 2   ♣ 7 3 2

(2)   **Dealer West : Both vulnerable**

WEST	NORTH	EAST	SOUTH
1♠	No	4♠	?

What should South do with :

♠ A J 2   ♡ - - -   ◊ K 10 6 3 2   ♣ K Q 6 4 3

Solutions

(1) Originally the spade void dampened South's enthusiasm. The bidding by the opponents, probably based on nine or ten hearts, gives partner a heart singleton or void. As North failed to show a pronounced black two-suiter over 2♡, South can reasonably expect North to have some diamonds and therefore a bid of 5◊ is not as reckless as it seems.

```
                        NORTH
                        ♠ K 10 9 8 7 4
                        ♡ - - -
                        ◊ K Q 9
                        ♣ A J 10 9
     ♠ J 2                              ♠ A Q 6 5 3
     ♡ Q J 8 7 6 2                      ♡ A K 10 4
     ◊ A 5                              ◊ 4
     ♣ K Q 6                            ♣ 8 5 4
                        SOUTH
                        ♠ - - - -
                        ♡ 9 5 3
                        ◊ J 10 8 7 6 3 2
                        ♣ 7 3 2
```

As the cards lie, 4♡ cannot be defeated and it takes a spade lead, ruffed, club to the ace and another spade ruff to beat 5♡. South's 5◊ is also unbeatable. On a heart lead, ruffed, declarer ruffs a spade, ruffs a heart, ruffs a spade, ruffs a heart, ruffs a spade and leads a trump. The club position makes it very easy.

If West starts with ace and another diamond, best for the defence, South needs to play well. Win the second diamond in dummy and lead the king of spades, ruffing East's ace. A club is led and declarer captures West's queen in dummy and ruffs a spade. Now a second club is led and declarer is able to set up the spades via a ruffing finesse. In fact, if West leads the ♠J originally, South can make twelve tricks.

(2) South's three spades indicates that North will have at most one spade and therefore is likely to hold length in at least one minor. South should bid 4NT, showing a two-suiter and North should bid the longer minor.

```
                     NORTH
                     ♠ - - -
                     ♡ 9 8 7 4
                     ◊ Q 9 5 4
                     ♣ A 10 9 8 5
   ♠ K Q 8 7 3                       ♠ 10 9 6 5 4
   ♡ A Q 6 3                         ♡ K J 10 5 2
   ◊ A J 7                           ◊ 8
   ♣ 2                               ♣ J 7
                     SOUTH
                     ♠ A J 2
                     ♡ - - -
                     ◊ K 10 6 3 2
                     ♣ K Q 6 4 3
```

If South bids 4NT, West may well double and North will bid 5♣. This cannot be beaten and if East fails to take the diamond ruff, North should make twelve tricks, on the bidding, by playing East for a singleton diamond after East turns up with a doubleton club.

If East-West bid on to 5♠ (it is not easy to find 5♡), South should double. Heart lead, ruffed, club to the ace, heart ruff leads to +500. The heart lead is no flight of fancy. As South is likely to have both minors and length in spades, North can place South with shortage in hearts.

Tip 20 : You can sometimes judge precisely the cost of a sacrifice.

Dealer North : Both vulnerable

WEST	NORTH	EAST	SOUTH
	1◊	No	1♠
4♡	Double (1)	No	4♠
?			

What action should West take with :

♠ 8 5   ♡ A K Q J 6 4 2   ◊ A K   ♣ 9 5

Solution :

It is pretty clear that West has nine tricks and that the sacrifice in 5♡ doubled will cost no more than 500. If partner can produce one trick, then you will be only minus 200. Attractive though these figures may be, West should choose to defend. Saving can be a poor investment.

                    NORTH
                    ♠ A 7
                    ♡ 3
                    ◊ Q J 7 4 3
                    ♣ A K Q J 8

♠ 8 5   ♠ Q 4 2
♡ A K Q J 6 4 2   ♡ 10 8
◊ A K   ◊ 10 8 6
♣ 9 5   ♣ 10 7 6 3 2

                    SOUTH
                    ♠ K J 10 9 6 3
                    ♡ 9 7 5
                    ◊ 9 5 2
                    ♣ 4

If East does have one trick for you, you can probably beat 4♠. As it is, East has no useful cards for a heart contract but 4♠ can still be defeated.

The flashy but risky defence of ◊A-K, low heart, diamond ruff is unnecessary. Cash ◊A-K followed by two top hearts and East scores a trump trick. The complete tip is :

You can sometimes judge precisely the cost of a sacrifice but do not save if you have a reasonable chance to defeat their contract.

Tip 21 : It is often best to lead low from a 4-card or longer unbid suit headed by the J-10. Leading the jack can cost.

From a suit headed by J-10-9 or J-10-8, it is standard to lead the jack. When the gap between the 10 and the next card is more than one card, it is usually best to lead low from a 4-card or longer suit unless partner has shown length in the suit. The lead of the jack from J-10-6-5 or similar is risky as it may collide with partner's K-Q or A-Q doubleton, potentially costing a trick. The jack lead from J-10-6-5-3-2 cost a slam in this position :

♣ A K 9

♣ J 10 6 5 3 2   ♣ Q

♣ 8 7 4

In 6♠, declarer had an inescapable outside loser as well as the losing club. West came to the rescue by leading the jack : Ace - Queen. Declarer later finessed dummy's 9 and landed the slam.

In similar fashion, the jack lead handed declarer 3NT on this deal :

Dealer West : Nil vulnerable

NORTH
♠ A 4 2
♡ K 8 7 4
♢ K 4 2
♣ A 9 5

WEST	EAST
♠ K 7	♠ 10 9 8 6
♡ J 10 6 5	♡ 9 3
♢ Q 8 3	♢ J 10 7 6
♣ J 8 3 2	♣ K Q 4

SOUTH
♠ Q J 5 3
♡ A Q 2
♢ A 9 5
♣ 10 7 6

After 1NT : 3NT, West led the jack of hearts. Declarer won with the ace and led a spade to the ace, and a spade back to the queen and king. Later the ♡Q dropped East's 9 and South finessed dummy's ♡8 for nine tricks. Had West led a low heart originally, declarer could not score four heart tricks.

Tip 22 : If the opponents bid to a slam after you have bid a suit, you can be certain that they are ready for a lead of your suit.

(1)   **Dealer South : Both vulnerable**

WEST	NORTH	EAST	SOUTH
			1♠
2♡	4♠	5♡	6♠
No	No	No	

What should West lead from :

♠ 3   ♡ A K J 9 3   ◇ K 8 7 2   ♣ J 6 2

(2)   **Dealer South : North-South vulnerable**

WEST	NORTH	EAST	SOUTH
			2♠ (1)
3♡	4♡ (2)	No	4♠
No	4NT (3)	No	5◇ (4)
No	5♡ (5)	No	5NT (6)
No	6♠	All pass	

(1) Weak two (2) Cue-bid in support of spades
(3) Roman Key Card Blackwood (4) One key card
(5) Asks for the ♠Q (6) 'Yes, I have the queen of trumps.'

What should West lead from :

♠ 8 5 4   ♡ Q J 8 7 6 5 4   ◇ - - -   ♣ K J 3

Solutions

(1) It may seem routine to place a top heart on the table but you can rest assured that a heart lead will not defeat the contract. Either South has a singleton in hearts or South can tell from the bidding that North is short in hearts. Given the weakness implied by North's bid, there is every chance that South is void in hearts and has a pronounced two-suiter.

While opening leads do not come with guarantees, your best shot is a low diamond. That needs less help from partner than any other start. In practice a heart was led and 6♠ made as the North-South cards were :

NORTH   ♠ K 10 7 6 2   ♡ 8 7 4   ◊ Q 9 5 3   ♣ 7

SOUTH   ♠ A J 9 8 5 4   ♡ - - -   ◊ 10 6   ♣ A K Q 8 5

The diamond lead could have brought instant success. Another point in favour of diamonds is that if South has jumped to slam on a strong two-suiter, the second suit is highly likely to be clubs as West has the ◊K.

As it was, declarer ruffed the heart lead and drew trumps in one fell swoop. Two of dummy's diamonds were discarded on the top clubs. Next came a club ruff, a heart ruff and a third diamond was pitched on South's fifth club. Declarer lost just one diamond trick.

(2) The deal arose in the 1993 Middle East Open Teams Championship won by India, with Egypt second and South Africa third.

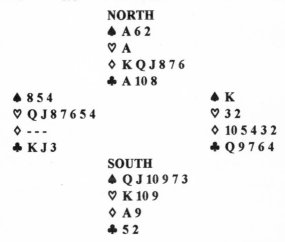

NORTH
♠ A 6 2
♡ A
◊ K Q J 8 7 6
♣ A 10 8

♠ 8 5 4
♡ Q J 8 7 6 5 4
◊ - - -
♣ K J 3

♠ K
♡ 3 2
◊ 10 5 4 3 2
♣ Q 9 7 6 4

SOUTH
♠ Q J 10 9 7 3
♡ K 10 9
◊ A 9
♣ 5 2

Thirteen tricks were regularly made in contracts of 4♠, 5♠ and 6♠ after a heart lead, many choosing a false card in the hope of scoring a diamond ruff. Declarer laid down the ♠A at trick 2 and had no further problems.

After the given auction West, K. A. Bani Amin of Bangladesh, felt sure North had hearts under control and so he led the ♣3. Having taken the ♣A, declarer's normal play is to take the spade finesse. Accordingly, declarer led a diamond to the ace. West ruffed, cashed the ♣K and continued with the ♣J. South ruffed, took the spade finesse and was three down after East gave West another diamond ruff. Great lead, Mr. Bani Amin.

Tip 23 : Playing against a relay pair, you are usually told the exact hand pattern of one of the hands. If their contract is 3NT and the revealed pattern includes a singleton or void, the hand opposite is almost always well-heeled in the short suit.

You are West on lead against 3NT with this collection :

♠ A 8 4 2   ♡ A K 8 3   ◇ Q 9 5 3   ♣ 7

Your opponents' relays have revealed that North, the dummy, will have at least 13 points with a 4-3-1-5 pattern (4 spades, 3 hearts, 1 diamond, 5 clubs). You know nothing about declarer's pattern. What do you lead?

Solution

As declarer figures to be covered in diamonds, your best chance is likely to be in dummy's 3-card holding, hearts. This was the full deal from the final of the 1990 World Teams between the USA and Germany :

```
                    NORTH
                    ♠ Q J 9 5
                    ♡ Q 10 5
                    ◇ 10
                    ♣ A 9 5 4 3
   ♠ A 8 4 2                        ♠ 10 3
   ♡ A K 8 3                        ♡ J 6 4 2
   ◇ Q 9 5 3                        ◇ K J 7 2
   ♣ 7                             ♣ 8 6 2
                    SOUTH
                    ♠ K 7 6
                    ♡ 9 7
                    ◇ A 8 6 4
                    ♣ K Q J 10
```

At one table the USA North-South scored +130 in 3♣. At the other the USA West started with ♡K, ♡A and a third heart. Declarer knocked out the ♠A and had nine tricks, +600. A diamond lead would have worked well this time but the holding opposite the known singleton is usually as solid as the Rock of Gibraltar. Had West started with the standard fourth-highest from A-K-x-x against no-trumps, declarer would have probably ducked in dummy and lost to the ♡J. Declarer could then be held to six tricks for +300.

Tip 24 : Be specific about the suit requested by a Lightner double. This avoids the disaster when partner has to guess and picks the wrong suit.

Dealer West : North-South vulnerable

WEST	NORTH	EAST	SOUTH
No	1◊	4♡	4♠
5♡	6♡	No	7♠
No	No	Double	All pass

What should West lead from :

♠ 9 7 6　　♡ Q 5 4　　◊ K 5　　♣ 9 7 4 3 2

Solution

The double of a non-sacrifice slam by the player not on lead asks for an unusual lead (not a trump, not a suit bid by the defenders). When made by a pre-empter, a Lightner double is often based on a void and a desire to ruff. On that basis, West would be inclined to choose a club lead. Regular partnerships are advised to be more specific. Use the Lightner slam double to ask unconditionally for partner to *lead the first suit bid by dummy*.

This was the actual deal from the 1995 US Life Masters Pairs :

```
                  ♠ 8 5 4 2
                  ♡ - - -
                  ◊ A Q J 10 9 6 4 2
                  ♣ A
   WEST                              EAST
   ♠ 9 7 6                           ♠ J 10
   ♡ Q 5 4                           ♡ A K 8 6 3 2
   ◊ K 5                             ◊ - - -
   ♣ 9 7 4 3 2                       ♣ Q J 10 6 5
                  ♠ A K Q 3
                  ♡ J 10 9 7
                  ◊ 8 7 3
                  ♣ K 8
```

Playing specific Lightner, West leads a diamond and 7♠ is one down at least. At the table West, playing general Lightner, led a club. South drew trumps and, placing East with a diamond void because of the double, took the diamond finesse. Making 7♠ doubled meant that South's courageous/foolhardy 4♠ bid would be forgiven.

Tip 25 : It is normally a losing strategy to lead away from an ace-high suit in a trump contract. In the long run you tend to lose more tricks than you gain. The best chance for success in leading away from an ace occurs when dummy has shown a strong balanced hand.

Dealer West : Both vulnerable

WEST	NORTH	EAST	SOUTH
No	2NT	No	3♣
No	3NT	No	4♡
No	No	No	

2NT = 21-22 balanced. 3♣ = Stayman and 3NT showed 4-4 in the majors.

What should West lead from :

♠ 10 9 8   ♡ 8   ◇ A 7 6 3 2   ♣ 10 5 4 2

Solution

Leading from an ace-high suit lacking the king against a trump contract is in general a dangerous pursuit, especially when declarer may well hold the king in the suit led. These are layouts that cost :

7 5

A 9 8 3   Q J 10 4

K 6 2

If West leads the suit, South scores a trick. If West stays off the suit, South cannot score a trick with the king.

Q 7 5

A 9 8 3   J 10 4

K 6 2

If West leads the suit, South scores two tricks. If West does not lead the suit, South can score only one trick.

Leading from an ace can work if partner has the king. As the opponents are likely to have more points than your side, the chance that partner has the king is less than one in three. Therefore, Rule 1 says, 'Do not lead an ace-high suit in a trump contract unless you hold the king also.' Rule 2 says, 'If you break Rule 1, lead the ace, not a low card.' That is to prevent a calamity such as this :

7

A 9 8 3   Q J 10 4 3

K 6 5

If West leads the suit, South scores the king. If West leads the ace, West makes one trick, South makes one. If West leads low, South makes one trick but West makes none, as South ruffs the losers in dummy.

When dummy has shown a strong balanced hand, leading away from an ace in a trump contract has better chances. Dummy is likely to hold the king and declarer may misguess a K-J combination. The problem lead arose in the 1989 Bermuda Bowl between France and Australia. West chose a low diamond and this helped to push declarer to defeat.

```
                    NORTH
                    ♠ A K J 6
                    ♥ K 6 4 2
                    ◊ K Q 10
                    ♣ A J
  ♠ 10 9 8                        ♠ Q 5
  ♥ 8                             ♥ Q 10 5
  ◊ A 7 6 3 2                     ◊ J 9 8
  ♣ 10 5 4 2                      ♣ K Q 9 6 3
                    SOUTH
                    ♠ 7 4 3 2
                    ♥ A J 9 7 3
                    ◊ 5 4
                    ♣ 8 7
```

On the ◊2 lead, dummy's king won. After ♥K and a heart to the ace, declarer led a second diamond. West ducked smoothly and declarer inserted the 10, losing to the jack. East shifted to the ♣K, taken by the ace. Declarer ruffed the ◊Q and exited with a club.

East cashed the ♥Q and with a perfect count of declarer's hand, continued with a club, giving declarer a useless ruff-and-discard. The French declarer naturally enough took the spade finesse. One down.

4♥ played by North is unbeatable, although four declarers did fail. Say East leads a top club (best). Declarer takes the ace and returns a club. East wins and has to help declarer. After a diamond to the ace and a spade return, declarer can cash ♥K and ♥A, followed by the diamond winners, discarding one spade. Now the heart exit endplays East once more and declarer loses no spade trick.

Tip 26 : Be prepared to do the unexpected.

Dealer West : E-W vulnerable

WEST	NORTH	EAST	SOUTH
1♠	2♣	No	2♦
No	3♦	No	3NT
No	No	No	

What should West lead from :

♠ J 9 8 7 6   ♡ A Q 7 4   ◊ A 7 6   ♣ 9

Solution

When the opponents have bid 3NT after you have mentioned a suit, they are usually prepared for that lead. If you have a second suit which has not been mentioned, they may not be ready for that.

En route to winning the 1995 Australian Grand National Teams, David Beauchamp did the right thing on this deal :

```
                    NORTH
                    ♠ A 4 2
                    ♡ J 2
                    ◊ 10 8 4
                    ♣ A K 7 4 3
♠ J 9 8 7 6                        ♠ 5 3
♡ A Q 7 4                          ♡ K 10 9 8 6
◊ A 7 6                            ◊ 5 3
♣ 9                               ♣ J 8 5 2
                    SOUTH
                    ♠ K Q 10
                    ♡ 5 3
                    ◊ K Q J 9 2
                    ♣ Q 10 6
```

After the heart lead, the defence took the first six tricks. If a spade is led initially, the contract can still be defeated (West must rise with the ace when South leads a low diamond at trick 2), but that would not be so if South had started with ♠K-Q-10-x or if South had K-x in hearts and East had J-10-x-x-x. As you are playing East for length in hearts, starting with a top heart is a good idea in case East has ♡J-6-5-3-2.

Tip 27 : It is not usually a good idea to lead a false card but it may be sensible in order to avoid tipping your hand to declarer or if you wish to deflect partner from the suit led.

(1)   **Dealer East : Both vulnerable**

WEST	NORTH	EAST	SOUTH
		No	1♡
2♣	2♡	4♣	4♡
No	No	No	

What should West lead from :

        ♠ A Q 9   ♡ 7 2   ◊ 7 3   ♣ K Q J 7 3 2

(2)   **Dealer South : Both vulnerable**

WEST	NORTH	EAST	SOUTH
			1NT
No	2♣	No	2◊
No	3NT	All pass	

1NT = 15-17; 2♣ = simple Stayman; 2◊ = no major

What should West lead from :

        ♠ 8 5 3 2   ♡ K Q J 8   ◊ 8 2   ♣ 7 6 4

Solutions

It is clear that there are few club tricks coming for your side. If partner gains the lead early, you would like your partner to shift to a spade. What is clear to you may not be nearly so obvious to partner.

You can hardly be blamed for making the standard lead of the king of clubs but if dummy has two low cards in clubs and partner has A-x-x-x, partner may decide to let your king hold. That could be fatal but it is not fair to blame partner. After all, partner does not know you started with six clubs. Since you would rather beat the contract than win the *post mortem*, it is not a bad move to start with the *queen* of clubs.

The complete deal :

NORTH
- ♠ 8 7 3
- ♥ J 10 8 5
- ♦ K Q 6 4
- ♣ 8 5

WEST
- ♠ A Q 9
- ♥ 7 2
- ♦ 7 3
- ♣ K Q J 7 3 2

EAST
- ♠ J 10 4 2
- ♥ Q
- ♦ 10 9 8 2
- ♣ A 10 6 4

SOUTH
- ♠ K 6 5
- ♥ A K 9 6 4 3
- ♦ A J 5
- ♣ 9

If West leads the king of clubs, there is a good case for East overtaking and switching to the jack of spades, but you would not want to bet your life on East finding that play. If East ducks the first club, declarer is home. If West leads the queen of clubs, East places the king with South and grabs the ace at once. Now it is simple to produce the spade switch.

(2) Even though North had used Stayman, Peter Schaltz of Denmark elected to lead a heart on this deal from the 1995 European Open Teams Championship. After all, North might have been looking for spades.

NORTH
- ♠ 10 7 4
- ♥ A 10 4 3
- ♦ K 5
- ♣ Q J 9 3

WEST
- ♠ 8 5 3 2
- ♥ K Q J 8
- ♦ 8 2
- ♣ 7 6 4

EAST
- ♠ Q J 9
- ♥ 7 6 5
- ♦ A Q 10 6 4 3
- ♣ 2

SOUTH
- ♠ A K 6
- ♥ 9 2
- ♦ J 9 7
- ♣ A K 10 8 5

Just in case dummy did turn up with A-10-x-x in hearts, Schaltz led the queen of hearts even though the partnership agreement was to lead top from sequences. Declarer took the ace of hearts, cashed two rounds of clubs ending in hand and led a diamond to the king and ace.

East, Dorthe Schaltz, placed South with A-K in clubs, the king of hearts and the jack of diamonds. As South could not also hold A-K in spades, West figured to hold one top spade. Accordingly, Dorthe switched to the queen of spades. South won with the ace and West discouraged. Declarer played a club to dummy and led the 5 of diamonds. East took the queen and exited with a heart to West's jack. This was the end-position :

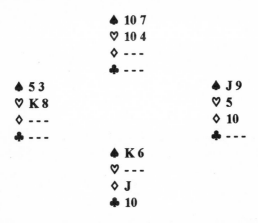

The defence had taken three tricks and declarer had enough tricks as soon as he regained the lead. Pursuing the deception from trick 1, Peter continued with the 8 of hearts. Expecting the ♡K to be with East, declarer played low from dummy. Whether East now held ♡K bare or ♡K-5, the hearts would now be blocked and at most one heart would be lost. The ♡8 won the trick and West's ♡K (surprise, surprise) was the coup de grace.

At the other table the Danish East led a diamond against North's 3NT and so presented declarer with his ninth trick instantly. Dorthe and Peter Schaltze won the Best Defence Award at the 1995 European Championships for this deal.

Tip 28 : Before you make your opening lead, try to envisage the shape of opposing hands. Sometimes knowing the probable shape of one of the hands can point the way to the best lead.

(1) **Dealer West : Both vulnerable**

WEST	NORTH	EAST	SOUTH
No	1♦	No	1♠
No	2♡	No	2♠
No	No	No	

What should West lead from :

♠ Q 9 8 7   ♡ Q 3   ♦ J 7 5   ♣ K J 9 4

(2) **Dealer East : Both vulnerable**

WEST	NORTH	EAST	SOUTH
		No	No
1♠	Double	4♠	4NT
No	5♣	No	5♦
No	No	No	

What should West lead from :

♠ A K J 10 9   ♡ K 5 4 2   ♦ - - -   ♣ K 9 7 4

Solutions

(1)

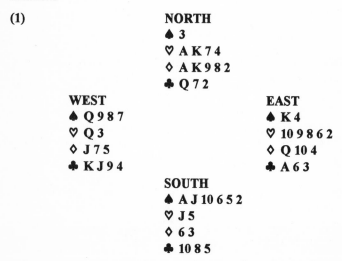

```
                    NORTH
                    ♠ 3
                    ♡ A K 7 4
                    ♦ A K 9 8 2
                    ♣ Q 7 2
   WEST                              EAST
   ♠ Q 9 8 7                         ♠ K 4
   ♡ Q 3                             ♡ 10 9 8 6 2
   ♦ J 7 5                           ♦ Q 10 4
   ♣ K J 9 4                         ♣ A 6 3
                    SOUTH
                    ♠ A J 10 6 5 2
                    ♡ J 5
                    ♦ 6 3
                    ♣ 10 8 5
```

Australian international star, Bob Richman, found the devastating lead of the *jack* of clubs. On a low club lead, declarer would play low in dummy and lose just two clubs and two or three spades. The ♣J was covered by the queen and ace and East returned a club. Richman scored two more club tricks and continued with the thirteenth club. East ruffed with the king of spades, an uppercut which gave the defence three trump tricks to take the contract one down.

West reasoned that North had shown a strong hand with 5-4 in diamonds and hearts. With three spades and one club, North would certainly have raised spades and with a 2-2 residue, North might still have raised. There was every chance that dummy would turn up with a 1-4-5-3 pattern and with the great disparity in strength, North was more likely to hold the ♣Q (see Tip 38). South was bound to have some clubs and if they included the 10, the lead of the surrounding jack might be essential.

(2)

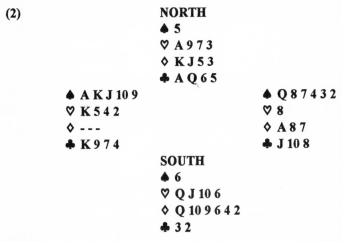

NORTH
♠ 5
♡ A 9 7 3
◊ K J 5 3
♣ A Q 6 5

WEST
♠ A K J 10 9
♡ K 5 4 2
◊ - - -
♣ K 9 7 4

EAST
♠ Q 8 7 4 3 2
♡ 8
◊ A 8 7
♣ J 10 8

SOUTH
♠ 6
♡ Q J 10 6
◊ Q 10 9 6 4 2
♣ 3 2

At the table West led a top spade and that was the end of the defence. If choosing that lead, West would have done better to sacrifice in 5♠.

South's 4NT and removal to 5◊ shows length in diamonds and hearts. North's double of 1♠ implies four hearts. North-South might well have nine hearts, giving East a void. Is it so hard to imagine heart lead ruffed, spade to West, heart lead ruffed? East's jump to 4♠ including a singleton or void, is further evidence of shortage in hearts. As it happens East has a singleton heart, but a heart lead by West is still the key to defeating 5◊.

Tip 29 : When partner makes an impossible bid in a competitive auction, be gracious and assume partner is rational. It is quite likely that partner is trying to focus your attention on a particular suit.

(1) **Dealer West : Nil vulnerable**

WEST	NORTH	EAST	SOUTH
3◊	3NT	5◊	5♠
No	No	5NT	No
6◊	6♠	All pass	

What should West lead from :

♠ J 7 2   ♡ K   ◊ Q 9 7 5 4 3 2   ♣ 10 9

(2) **Dealer South : Both vulnerable**

WEST	NORTH	EAST	SOUTH
			1♠
No	2◊	3♣	3♠
5♣	5♠	6♣	No
No	6♠	All pass	

What should West lead from :

♠ 6 2   ♡ Q 7 6 5 2   ◊ J 6 4   ♣ K Q 2

Solutions

(1)

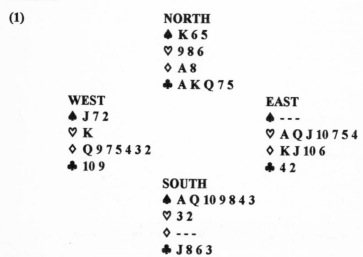

```
                        NORTH
                        ♠ K 6 5
                        ♡ 9 8 6
                        ◊ A 8
                        ♣ A K Q 7 5
        WEST                            EAST
        ♠ J 7 2                         ♠ - - -
        ♡ K                             ♡ A Q J 10 7 5 4
        ◊ Q 9 7 5 4 3 2                 ◊ K J 10 6
        ♣ 10 9                          ♣ 4 2
                        SOUTH
                        ♠ A Q 10 9 8 4 3
                        ♡ 3 2
                        ◊ - - -
                        ♣ J 8 6 3
```

Having jumped to 5◊ originally, East cannot have any legitimate grand slam aspirations. 5NT makes no sense as a natural bid or as a bid suggesting slam ambitions. What then can it mean?

Had East bid 6♣ instead of 5NT, that would have been easily recognisable as lead-directing for clubs. In the 1995 Australian National Butler Pairs, Warren Lazer produced the highly imaginative 5NT which stumped a number of top players at the time. Since 6♣ asks for a club, 5NT asks for the suit that could not be bid conveniently, hearts. It takes the heart lead to defeat 6♠. On any other lead, declarer has thirteen tricks. East might have bid 4♡ earlier but that does not detract from the brilliancy of 5NT.

(2)

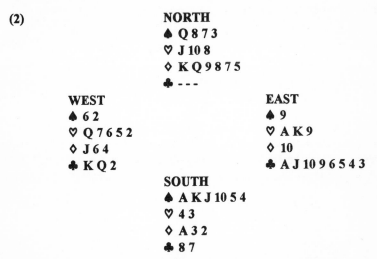

```
                        NORTH
                        ♠ Q 8 7 3
                        ♡ J 10 8
                        ◊ K Q 9 8 7 5
                        ♣ - - -
        WEST                            EAST
        ♠ 6 2                           ♠ 9
        ♡ Q 7 6 5 2                     ♡ A K 9
        ◊ J 6 4                         ◊ 10
        ♣ K Q 2                         ♣ A J 10 9 6 5 4 3
                        SOUTH
                        ♠ A K J 10 5 4
                        ♡ 4 3
                        ◊ A 3 2
                        ♣ 8 7
```

One would have thought that a 5NT lead-directing bid had little scope but it surfaced again on the above deal from the 1995 Bermuda Bowl. After the given bidding, the South African West led the ♣K and the Canadian declarer had thirteen tricks, +1460.

West might have applied Tip 22 (*slam-bidding opponents are ready for the lead of your bid suit*) to find the killing heart lead, but East also missed an opportunity. Foreseeing the possibility that North-South might bid 6♠ when he bid 6♣, East could have used the Lazer 5NT bid to say, 'Please bid 6♣ but if they bid 6♠, lead the suit I cannot show.' As East's double of 6♠ would ask for a diamond lead (dummy's first bid suit — see Tip 24), the 5NT bid must ask partner to lead the unbid suit, hearts.

Tip 30 : From suits headed by Q-J-10 or Q-J-9, the queen is the standard start. From weaker Q-J-x-x or longer suits, lead the queen if partner is marked with length in the suit or if declarer has shown a very strong balanced hand. Otherwise leading low is often better.

The problem with Q-J-x-x or longer is that you will not always be right whichever approach you take. Leading the queen works well here :

K 10

Q J 6 5 2   A 9 8 3

7 4

Lead the queen and declarer has no tricks. Lead a low card and declarer can score a trick by playing low in dummy. The same follows if dummy has something like K-7 and declarer 10-4

However, there is also a downside to leading the queen. Lead the queen in this layout and you have just blocked the suit.

8 7 3

Q J 6 5 2   K 4

A 10 9

This could cost even in a trump contract. If West leads the queen and East plays the king, the defence takes only one trick. If East plays low, South can take the ace and if West's only entry is dislodged before the suit is unravelled, the defence again comes to only one trick.

7 3

Q J 6 5   A K 2

10 9 8 4

If West leads the queen in no-trumps, the defence cannot conveniently collect their four tricks.

K 10 8

Q J 6 5 2   9 3

A 7 4

Lead the queen and declarer wins with the ace and finesses the 10 later for three tricks. Lead low and declarer is likely to play dummy's 8, hoping for West to have led from Q-9-x-x or J-9-x-x. If so, declarer scores only two tricks.

If partner has shown length in the suit, lead the queen. If declarer has shown a powerful balanced hand such as opening 2NT or rebidding with a jump in no-trumps, lead the queen. Declarer may well have A-K-10. Otherwise, lead low from Q-J-x-x or longer suits missing the 10 and 9.

Tip 31 : In a trump contract after a low card lead, if the opposition do not take the ace at trick 1, they are planning a ruff in the suit led.

Dealer West : Nil vulnerable

WEST		EAST	
♠ A Q 7		♠ 8 3	
♡ Q 8 6 2		♡ K 10 9 5 4 3	
◊ A 7 3		◊ K 8	
♣ K Q 3		♣ 9 8 7	

WEST	NORTH	EAST	SOUTH
1NT (1)	No	2◊ (2)	No
2♡	No	3♡ (3)	No
4♡	No	No	No

(1) 15-18   (2) Transfer   (3) 6+ hearts and inviting game

North leads 6 of clubs, South plays the 10. Plan the play for West.

Solution

NORTH
♠ K 10 9 5 4
♡ A 7
◊ Q 10 9 5
♣ 6 2

♠ A Q 7		♠ 8 3
♡ Q 8 6 2		♡ K 10 9 5 4 3
◊ A 7 3		◊ K 8
♣ K Q 3		♣ 9 8 7

SOUTH
♠ J 6 2
♡ J
◊ J 6 4 2
♣ A J 10 5 4

If West leads a trump at trick 2, North wins and plays the second club to the ace and ruffs the club return. Declarer loses a spade later. One down.

Foreseeing the danger, Australian international Tina Zines, in a national teams event, played ◊K, ◊A and a diamond ruff before leading a trump. After ruffing the club, North was endplayed and there was no spade loser.

Tip 32 : Even though standard technique offers you excellent chances, always take any enemy bidding into account when forming your plan of play.

Dealer North: N-S vulnerable

WEST		EAST	
♠ A K 10 7 4		♠ Q 9 8 6	
♥ 8 3		♥ J	
◊ J 10 5 4		◊ A 9 6 3	
♣ 3 2		♣ A Q J 7	

WEST	NORTH	EAST	SOUTH
	No	1◊	2♥ (1)
Double	3♥	Double (2)	No
4♠	No	No	No

(1) Intermediate, 11-15 points   (2) Game invitation

North leads the king of hearts. How would you play as West if North :

(a) continues with a heart

(b) switches to a trump

(c) switches to the 5 of clubs

(d) switches to the 8 of diamonds

Solution

Taking the club finesse and two diamond finesses will work most of the time. If North holds any of the three critical cards you are home.

The bidding and the opening lead suggest things may not be so smooth. North's ♥K lead is presumably from some K-Q holding. That gives South only the ace in hearts and as South has advertised the equivalent of an opening hand, it should come as no surprise if South in fact does hold the three critical cards in diamonds and clubs.

If trumps are 3-1, by all means take all three finesses, starting with the club finesse. Other routes are not safe. However if trumps are 2-2 and the breaks in the minor suits are normal, you can almost guarantee your game.

This was the complete deal :

```
                        NORTH
                        ♠ 5 3
                        ♡ K Q 6 5
                        ◊ 8 2
                        ♣ 9 8 6 5 4
        ♠ A K 10 7 4                    ♠ Q 9 8 6
        ♡ 8 3                           ♡ J
        ◊ J 10 5 4                      ◊ A 9 6 3
        ♣ 3 2                           ♣ A Q J 7
                        SOUTH
                        ♠ J 2
                        ♡ A 10 9 7 4 2
                        ◊ K Q 7
                        ♣ K 10
```

(a) If North continues with a heart, ruff in dummy, draw trumps ending in hand and take the club finesse. South wins and returns a club. Discard a diamond on a club winner and ruff dummy's last club. Run the ◊J and endplay South.

(b) If North switches to a trump, the play is essentially the same. Win the spade in hand, ruff your heart and lead a second spade to hand, drawing trumps. Take the club finesse and continue as in (a).

(c) If North switches to a club, finesse the queen. Win the return, draw trumps, ruff the heart loser, eliminate the clubs and endplay South in diamonds as before.

(d) The diamond shift at trick 2 destroys the diamond endplay but does not save the defenders. Duck the diamond to South and win, say, the trump return in hand. Ruff the heart and draw the last trump. Then lead another diamond. If North has played high-low in diamonds, trust North to have started with a doubleton. Rise with the ace of diamonds and exit with a diamond. South has to lead a club or give you a ruff-and-discard.

If North has played low-high in diamonds, you will have to judge whether to play North for Honour-x-x or South for K-Q doubleton.

Tip 33 : When you are in desperate trouble, try to find some deceptive stroke to put the defenders off their stride.

(1)   **Dealer North: N-S vulnerable**

WEST			EAST
♠ A 10 8			♠ Q 4 3
♡ Q 8 3			♡ J 2
◊ 10 3			◊ K Q J 8 5 4
♣ A Q 7 4 2			♣ K 3

WEST	NORTH	EAST	SOUTH
	No	1◊	1♡
2♣	No	2◊	No
2♡ (1)	No	3◊	No
3NT	No	No	No

(1) Strong hand, asking for a stopper in hearts

With poor holdings in both majors and no aces, East's opening bid is no thing of beauty but favourable vulnerability brings out the lion in the most timid of mice. Although West's sequence expressed doubt about 3NT (a jump to 3NT over 2◊ would have been more adamant), East passed 3NT in the hope that West had the ◊A.

North leads the 9 of hearts. Plan West's play.

(2)   **Dealer West : Both vulnerable**

WEST			EAST
♠ A K 10 7			♠ Q 5 4 3
♡ Q J 7 5			♡ K 9 3
◊ Q 7			◊ 10 5 2
♣ A K Q			♣ 10 4 3

WEST	NORTH	EAST	SOUTH
2NT	No	3NT	All pass

4♠ would have been an easier task but it's too late to worry about that now. North leads the 4 of hearts : low from dummy, 10 from South. How should West plan the play?

(1)

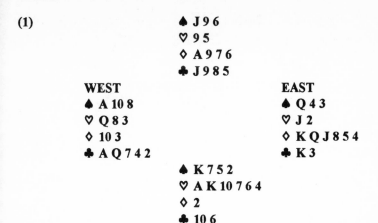

It is easy enough to defeat 3NT. South simply ducks the first heart. Australian international and winner of many national championships, Bob Richman, induced a defensive error by playing the ♡J from dummy. As the ♡9 lead meant South had A-K in hearts, the ♡J could not cost and players tend to cover honours instinctively. South should still have ducked but he took his eye off the ball and played the ♡K. End of the defence.

(2)

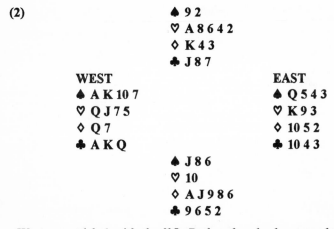

West won trick 1 with the ♡Q. Rather than lead a second heart and risk a signal from South, declarer crossed to the ♠Q and led a gutsy diamond to the queen. North took the king and, hoping South had started with J-10-x in hearts, obliged by leading another low heart.

Tip 34 : Study the methods used by the opponents. They often provide a wealth of information which you can use in working out the patterns and holdings in the unseen hands.

(1)　　　　　　　　**Dealer South : Nil vulnerable**

	WEST		EAST
	♠ 2		♠ K J 10 9 4 3
	♡ A K 6 4 3 2		♡ - - -
	◇ K		◇ Q 10 9 8
	♣ K Q 9 8 5		♣ 6 4 2

WEST	NORTH	EAST	SOUTH
			1◇ (1)
1♡	2◇ (2)	No	No
3♣	No	No	No

The opponents are playing a strong 1♣ system. They explain their bids as follows :

(1) 1◇ = 11-12 points balanced with no 4-card major *OR* 11-15 points with 4+ diamonds, 4+ clubs and no 4-card major

(2) 2◇ = 5+ diamonds, not forcing

North leads ♣7. South takes ♣A and returns ♣3. Plan West's play.

(2)　　　　　　　　**Dealer South : Nil vulnerable**

	WEST		EAST
	♠ A 8 3		♠ K J 10 7 5 4
	♡ A 8		♡ J
	◇ A Q J 4		◇ - - -
	♣ A K J 10		♣ Q 9 7 5 4 3

WEST	NORTH	EAST	SOUTH
			No
1♣ (1)	2◇ (2)	2♠ (3)	No
2NT	No	4♣	No
7♣	No	No	No

(1) Artificial and strong (2) Weak jump-overcall. North-South play that overcalls at the one-level show weak two-suiters and jump-overcalls show weak one-suiters. (3) Natural and forcing to game.

North leads the 2 of clubs to which South follows. Plan the play.

(1) Since North has shown five diamonds, South cannot hold four diamonds. Therefore, the second option of the 1◊ opening does not exist on this deal.

Since South's 1◊ opening denies a 4-card major and North's 2◊ means that South cannot hold four diamonds, South's pattern has to be 3-3-3-4 after the club lead at trick 1. The reflex play on South's club return at trick 2 is the king of clubs but if the opponents are reliable, and those who play such precise methods generally are, it is perfectly safe to insert the 9 of clubs. This was the complete deal :

                    NORTH
                    ♠ 8 7 6
                    ♡ Q J 7 5
                    ◊ A J 7 4 3
                    ♣ 7
    WEST   **EAST**
    ♠ 2   ♠ K J 10 9 4 3
    ♡ A K 6 4 3 2   ♡ - - -
    ◊ K   ◊ Q 10 9 8
    ♣ K Q 9 8 5   ♣ 6 4 2
                    SOUTH
                    ♠ A Q 5
                    ♡ 10 9 8
                    ◊ 6 5 2
                    ♣ A J 10 3

After the ♣9 holds, ruff a low heart and come off the board with a diamond to the king and ace. As the cards lie and as long as declarer picks the position in spades and diamonds, there is nothing the defence can do. Declarer would lose at most one trick in each suit.

If declarer rises with a top club at trick 2, the defence can come to two club tricks as well as one trick in each of the other suits. One down. South could have ensured one down by returning the jack or ten of clubs at trick 2. You must make the most of this tiny slip.

(2) Given North's weak jump-overcall in diamonds, the natural inclination is to draw trumps and play South to hold the ♠Q. You will do better if you curb your instincts and pay attention as the play unfolds.

After winning the club lead in hand, ruff a low diamond in dummy, come to hand with a trump (South follows), and continue with ◊A and another diamond ruffed in dummy. South follows to three rounds of diamonds. A heart to the ace is followed by your last diamond, ruffed in dummy as South discards a heart. What can you deduce at this stage?

North has turned up with six diamonds and one club. North will not have started with five hearts. With a 6-5 pattern, North would have used some two-suited overcall rather than the weak jump-overcall to 2◊, especially with such a modest diamond suit. Note how you use your knowledge of the opponents' methods to piece together the missing cards and judge the likely hand patterns around the table. If North has fewer than five hearts, North must have at least two spades. Therefore you must not finesse against South on the second round of spades.

If South began with seven hearts, South might well have opened 3♡. Given South's failure to pre-empt, North is quite likely to hold four hearts and have a 2-4-6-1 pattern. This was the full deal :

NORTH
♠ Q 9
♡ 9 7 6 3
◊ K 10 6 5 3 2
♣ 2

WEST
♠ A 8 3
♡ A 8
◊ A Q J 4
♣ A K J 10

EAST
♠ K J 10 7 5 4
♡ J
◊ - - -
♣ Q 9 7 5 4 3

SOUTH
♠ 6 2
♡ K Q 10 5 4 2
◊ 9 8 7
♣ 8 6

Tip 35 : With Q-J-9-8-x in hand opposite dummy's A-x-x, you start by leading the queen. You should have a firm policy how to play this suit for no losers if everyone plays low on the first round, and also how to proceed if the queen is covered by the king.

Dealer East : Nil vulnerable

WEST		EAST
♠ K 7 2		♠ Q 9 8
♡ Q 9		♡ J 7
◊ Q J 9 8 3		◊ A 6 4
♣ A 7 2		♣ K Q J 10 9

WEST	NORTH	EAST	SOUTH
		1NT	2♡
3♣ (1)	3♡	No	No
Double (2)	No	4♣	All pass

(1) Transfer to diamonds (2) Co-operative double, shows values

North leads the ♡2 to South's ace and wins the heart return with the king. North shifts to ♠6 : 8 - 10 - King. West leads the ◊Q : 5 - 4 - 2. How should West continue? How should West play if it had gone ◊Q - King - Ace - 2?

Solution

	NORTH	
	♠ 6 5 4 3	
	♡ K 4 2	
	◊ K 7 5	
	♣ 8 6 3	

WEST		EAST
♠ K 7 2		♠ Q 9 8
♡ Q 9		♡ J 7
◊ Q J 9 8 3		◊ A 6 4
♣ A 7 2		♣ K Q J 10 9

	SOUTH	
	♠ A J 10	
	♡ A 10 8 6 5 3	
	◊ 10 2	
	♣ 5 4	

With holdings such as the diamonds, lead the queen. If all follow low, play second hand to have K-x-x and the other 10-x. Therefore lead the jack next. It is too hard for a defender with K-x to play low on the queen. If the queen is covered, play second hand to have K-x and fourth player 10-x-x.

Tip 36 : A lead-directing bid by an opponent can often enable you to place the missing high cards, especially those in the suit doubled.

Dealer West : Nil vulnerable

WEST		EAST	
♠ A Q		♠ 8 5	
♡ 10 4 3		♡ A Q 7 6	
◊ K J 10 9 6 2		◊ A Q 5 4	
♣ 7 2		♣ A J 3	

WEST	NORTH	EAST	SOUTH
1◊	No	1♡	No
2◊	No	3♣	Double
3♡	No	4♣	No
4♡	No	4NT	No
5◊	No	No	No

How should West plan the play if :

(a) North leads the jack of spades?

(b) North leads the 6 of clubs?

(c) North leads the 5 of hearts?

(d) North leads the 3 of diamonds?

Solution

3NT would have been much easier and in the 1995 Politiken World Pairs, Omar Sharif and Jose Damiani reached the best spot via No bid : 1NT, 3NT. Simple and effective. One would expect this to be the popular contract but the majority of pairs played in diamonds, making just ten tricks.

In the given auction, notwithstanding South's double of 3♣, East might have bid 3♠, fourth-suit, over 3♡. West would have welcomed the chance to bid 3NT because with that featherweight opening, West wants to discourage East from any thoughts of slam.

West in the above auction was Norway's young star, Geir Helgemo, who was the only one to make eleven tricks in diamonds. South's double of 3♣ guided Helgemo to the winning line.

                    NORTH
                    ♠ J 10 9 7 4 2
                    ♥ J 8 5
                    ◊ 3
                    ♣ 9 6 5

WEST   **EAST**
♠ A Q   ♠ 8 5
♥ 10 4 3   ♥ A Q 7 6
◊ K J 10 9 6 2   ◊ A Q 5 4
♣ 7 2   ♣ A J 3

                    SOUTH
                    ♠ K 6 3
                    ♥ K 9 2
                    ◊ 8 7
                    ♣ K Q 10 8 4

(a) Despite South's double, North led the jack of spades, won by the queen. The ♠A was cashed, followed by two rounds of trumps ending in dummy. Next came a low club. South grabbed the 10 and continued with the king. Declarer won with the ace and played back the jack of clubs. When South produced the expected queen, West did not ruff. He simply threw a heart and South was endplayed, forced into leading a heart into the A-Q or conceding a ruff-and-discard.

(b) On the ♣6 lead, declarer would duck in dummy, take the ♣K return with the ace, finesse the ♠Q, cash ♠A and ◊K, cross to the ◊A and lead the ♣J for the same outcome.

(c) On a low heart lead, duck in dummy and let it run to your ten. Whatever South does, declarer can make twelve tricks, losing just one heart and discarding the club loser on the thirteenth heart.

(d) If North leads the 3 of diamonds, win in dummy, take the spade finesse, cash ♠A, cross to ◊Q and lead the low club from dummy as in line (a). Even if South ducks this to North's 9, the defence is stymied.

Helgemo's line is an excellent one even without South's double. There is no rush to tackle the hearts. It is possible to add a bit more to Tip 36 :

With plenty of trumps in both hands, seek an endplay.

Tip 37 : Low level doubles for takeout are all the rage these days, almost regardless of the early auction. If you wind up as declarer after a takeout double, play the doubler to be short in the suit doubled.

(1)	WEST		EAST	
Dealer North	♠ J 6		♠ A 9 3	
Nil vulnerable	♡ K 10 6 3 2		♡ A J 7 4	
	◊ K J 3		◊ A 10 5 4 2	
	♣ 9 8 5		♣ 6	

WEST	NORTH	EAST	SOUTH
	No	1◊	Double*
1♡	1♠	3♡	No
4♡	No	No	No

North leads the 4 of spades. Plan West's play.

(2)	WEST		EAST	
Dealer North	♠ J 2		♠ A 10 9 4	
Nil vulnerable	♡ 9 8 4		♡ J 6 5	
	◊ A K J 8 6 4 3		◊ 9 5	
	♣ 6		♣ A 9 4 3	

WEST	NORTH	EAST	SOUTH
	1♡	No	1NT
2◊	Double*	No	3♣
3◊	No	No	No

North cashes the ace, king and queen of hearts. South discards the ♣8 on the third heart and North switches to the ♣Q. Plan the play for West.

(3)	WEST		EAST	
Dealer North	♠ A K 10 4		♠ 8 6 3	
Nil vulnerable	♡ Q 10 4		♡ 3	
	◊ 6 3		◊ A 8 4 2	
	♣ 9 8 6 5		♣ A Q J 10 3	

WEST	NORTH	EAST	SOUTH
	No	1♣	Double*
1♠	2♡	2♠	No
No	Double*	All pass	

North leads ♡6. South wins with ♡A and switches to ♠5. Plan the play.

*Takeout double

(1) Declarer should take dummy's ♠A and continue with ♡A and a heart to the 10 if the ♡Q has not yet appeared. South's takeout double of 1◊ implies length in the other suits. Play South for Q-x-x in hearts rather than x-x. In diamonds, cash ◊K and continue with ◊J, letting the jack run if North plays low. As South doubled 1◊, South figures to be short in diamonds. Assume the ◊Q is with the greater length. Pick both red suits and you have eleven tricks. Get them both wrong and you fail.

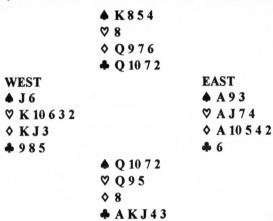

```
                        ♠ K 8 5 4
                        ♡ 8
                        ◊ Q 9 7 6
                        ♣ Q 10 7 2
         WEST                              EAST
         ♠ J 6                             ♠ A 9 3
         ♡ K 10 6 3 2                      ♡ A J 7 4
         ◊ K J 3                           ◊ A 10 5 4 2
         ♣ 9 8 5                           ♣ 6
                        ♠ Q 10 7 2
                        ♡ Q 9 5
                        ◊ 8
                        ♣ A K J 4 3
```

(2) As North doubled 2◊ for takeout, play North to be short in diamonds. Take the ♣A, lead a diamond to the ace, cross to the ♠A and finesse the ◊J.

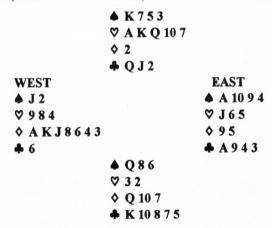

```
                        ♠ K 7 5 3
                        ♡ A K Q 10 7
                        ◊ 2
                        ♣ Q J 2
         WEST                              EAST
         ♠ J 2                             ♠ A 10 9 4
         ♡ 9 8 4                           ♡ J 6 5
         ◊ A K J 8 6 4 3                   ◊ 9 5
         ♣ 6                               ♣ A 9 4 3
                        ♠ Q 8 6
                        ♡ 3 2
                        ◊ Q 10 7
                        ♣ K 10 8 7 5
```

That line is not a sure thing but it is the best bet after North's double.

(3) South's takeout double of 1♣ implies shortage in clubs, length in the other suits. North's double of 2♠ for takeout is based on shortage in spades. South's passing this double for penalties implies length and strength in spades.

Pursuing these thoughts declarer played the ♠10 on South's 5 and the ten held the trick. This was the full deal :

```
                    ♠ 2
                    ♡ K J 7 6 5
                    ◊ J 9 5
                    ♣ K 7 4 2
WEST                                    EAST
♠ A K 10 4                              ♠ 8 6 3
♡ Q 10 4                                ♡ 3
◊ 6 3                                   ◊ A 8 4 2
♣ 9 8 6 5                               ♣ A Q J 10 3
                    ♠ Q J 9 7 5
                    ♡ A 9 8 2
                    ◊ K Q 10 7
                    ♣ - - -
```

At trick 3 declarer ran the 9 of clubs, ruffed by South who continued with the queen of spades taken by the ace. A club was led to the 10 and South discarded a heart. A spade to the king was followed by another club finesse. South discarded a heart on this and then ruffed the ♣A. West came to eight tricks via four spades, three clubs and the ◊A.

South might have defeated the contract by ruffing the club at trick 5 and leading a heart to take out dummy's last trump. Declarer is stuck in dummy : after ◊A, South takes the next diamond and leads a heart to North, who plays a club for South to ruff. That gives the defence two hearts, a diamond and three club ruffs.

Even that would have been no triumph for North-South since 4♡ will make on many lines of play (a cross-ruff is easy after a spade lead if declarer scores a diamond trick and hearts are not led early). North might have bid 3♡ over 1♠ and South should pay heed to Tip 14 : **Do not leave a takeout double in for penalties if you can support partner.**

Tip 38 : When missing two significant honours in a suit, play the opponent with greater strength to hold the higher missing honour. When one opponent has significantly greater length than the other in one suit, the other is likely to hold greater length in other suits.

Dealer North: Both vulnerable

WEST			EAST
♠ Q 10 5 2			♠ A 9 6 4
♡ 9			♡ A 7 5
◇ A Q 10 7 6 4			◇ 9 8 5
♣ A 4			♣ J 7 6

WEST	NORTH	EAST	SOUTH
	No	No	2♣ (1)
2◇	No	3♣ (2)	Double
3♠	No	4♠	All pass

(1) Precision : 6+ clubs or 5+ clubs and a 4-card major
(2) Asking for a club stopper for 3NT

North leads the 9 of clubs : 6 - 10 - Ace. Plan West's play.

Solution

In the 1995 Bermuda Bowl, the USA and the Indonesian West both received a club lead, taken by the ace. Both continued with a spade to the ace and a second spade. This was the trump layout :

♠ J 8 3

♠ Q 10 5 2   ♠ A 9 6 4

♠ K 7

South who had started with ♠K 7 ♡Q 10 6 2 ◇K ♣K Q 10 5 3 2 won with ♠K, cashed ♣K and continued with ♣Q, promoting North's ♠J. The inescapable diamond loser meant one down.

On the bidding South is more likely to hold ♠K than North and South's 6+ club length meant North would be more likely to hold length in spades. The actual trump position was reasonably foreseeable.

The winning play is heroic but plausible, though not certain by any means : take the ♣A and run the ♠10 to South's king. Ruff the third club with the ♠Q, finesse dummy's ♠9 and draw the last trump. This holds the losers to one spade, one diamond and one club.

Tip 39 : Beware of the defender who attacks dummy's long suit.

(1)   **Dealer East: Nil vulnerable**

	WEST		EAST
	♠ K Q 10 9 4 3		♠ A J 8
	♡ K 4 3		♡ 7 5
	◇ 8 5		◇ A Q J 9 6 2
	♣ A 3		♣ J 5

WEST	NORTH	EAST	SOUTH
		1◇	No
1♠	No	2◇	No
3♠	No	4♠	All pass

North leads the 7 of diamonds. Plan West's play.

(2)   **Dealer East: Nil vulnerable**

	WEST		EAST
	♠ K Q 10 9 4		♠ 7 3
	♡ 8 4 3		♡ K 7 5
	◇ 2		◇ A K 10 4 3
	♣ A 9 6 3		♣ K 10 4

WEST	NORTH	EAST	SOUTH
		1◇	No
1♠	No	1NT	No
2♠	No	No	No

North leads the ♡Q : what should West play from dummy?

As the lead marks the ♡A with South, West plays low from dummy at trick 1 and does the same on North's ♡J continuation. South produces the ♡A at trick 2 and switches to the jack of diamonds, taken by the ace. West plays a spade to the king which wins. How should West continue?

Solutions

1) At the table, declarer saw no danger in playing the queen of diamonds at trick 1. 'If the lead is not a singleton,' thought West, 'all is well. At most I will lose a diamond and two hearts. If it is a singleton, I am still all right. North can ruff the diamond return and perhaps play a heart to South's ace but then I can ruff the next diamond high. No problems.'

There was however a tiny flaw in West's thinking as South held :

♠ 6   ♡ Q J 8 6   ◊ K 10 4 3   ♣ Q 9 7 2

South took the ◊Q with the king and shifted to the ♡Q. If West ducked this, South would then give North the diamond ruff. In practice, West covered the king and North took the ace. A heart back to the jack and the diamond ruff polished off West's game. Such an outcome tends to turn declarer into a morose alcoholic, a sadder Budweiser man.

West should win with the ◊A at trick 1 and can lead the ◊Q next. Whether South takes this or not, West has a comfortable path to setting up the diamonds. North is also not free from blame. When dummy has shown a long suit, it is usually best to lead an unbid suit. An initial club lead allows the defence to defeat the contract legitimately.

(2)

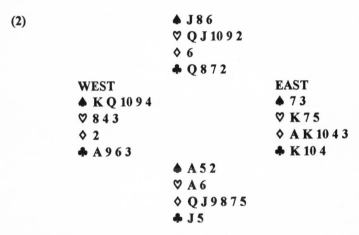

```
                    ♠ J 8 6
                    ♡ Q J 10 9 2
                    ◊ 6
                    ♣ Q 8 7 2
   WEST                              EAST
   ♠ K Q 10 9 4                      ♠ 7 3
   ♡ 8 4 3                           ♡ K 7 5
   ◊ 2                               ◊ A K 10 4 3
   ♣ A 9 6 3                         ♣ K 10 4
                    ♠ A 5 2
                    ♡ A 6
                    ◊ Q J 9 8 7 5
                    ♣ J 5
```

After trick 2 South is known to be out of hearts. West should be highly suspicious of that ◊J shift when a trump or a club would be much more appealing. A spade to the king marks South with the ♠A. If North had it he would have won and allowed South to ruff the ♡K.

Continue with the ♠Q. If South takes ♠A and leads a diamond, discard a club. Even if North ruffs with a low trump, West loses only three spades and two hearts. At the table, West did cross to the ♣K but tried to cash the ◊K, pitching a club. North ruffed and gave South the heart ruff. West still had to lose the ♠A and a club for one down. Another morose alcoholic.

Tip 40 : An opponent who fails to find the killing lead may also be unlikely to find the killing switch.

Dealer West : Nil vulnerable

WEST			EAST
♠ 6 5 2			♠ J 10 3
♡ Q 4			♡ K J 5
◊ A 10 2			◊ K 9 5 4 3
♣ K Q J 5 2			♣ A 3

WEST	NORTH	EAST	SOUTH
1NT (1)	No	3NT	All pass
(1) 12-14			

North leads the 10 of clubs, South plays the 4. Plan the play.

Solution

There are two competing lines : play a heart *OR* try to set up diamonds.

If you tackle hearts, South might have ♡A and have an easier time finding the spade shift. If North has ♡A, your failure to play diamonds suggests you need no tricks there. With South's discouraging ♣4, only spades are left.

Though no sure thing, winning with the ♣A and playing a diamond to the 10 has a lot going for it. If North had it tough finding the spade lead, you have done little to tip off North about your real fear. After winning with the ◊J it would take a genius North to play a spade next on this layout :

		♠ Q 7 4	
		♡ A 9 6 2	
		◊ J 8	
		♣ 10 9 8 7	
WEST			EAST
♠ 6 5 2			♠ J 10 3
♡ Q 4			♡ K J 5
◊ A 10 2			◊ K 9 5 4 3
♣ K Q J 5 2			♣ A 3
	♠ A K 9 8		
	♡ 10 8 7 3		
	◊ Q 7 6		
	♣ 6 4		

Tip 41 : When switching to K-x-x in a suit where you need at least four tricks quickly in no-trumps, lead the low card when you have no expectation of regaining the lead early. It may be necessary to play your second highest card if there is a danger of blocking the suit.

NORTH
10 2

WEST		EAST
A J 9 7		K 5 3

SOUTH
Q 8 6 4

East is on lead and the defence needs four tricks at once from this suit. If East plays king and another, South plays low and the defenders can take only three tricks. East should start with the 3, West winning with the jack when South plays low. West returns the 7 to East's king and the 5 from East mops up the suit with West's A-9 poised over South's Q-8.

9 2

WEST		EAST
A J 7 5		K 10 3

Q 8 6 4

As above, the defence needs four tricks quickly. If East plays king and 10, South can cover the ten and the limit is three tricks. If East leads the 3, South plays low and West wins with the jack. The 5 goes to East's king, but when East plays the 10, South can play low and the suit is blocked.

The solution is for East to start with the 10. If South ducks, the 10 wins, and king and another finish South off. If South covers with the queen, West wins with the ace, returns the 5 to East's king and the 3 up to West's J-7 punctures South's remaining 8-6.

10 7 6 3

WEST		EAST
K 9 2		A Q 8 4

J 5

Similarly here, West needs to start with the 9 even though East might be deceived. No other card allows the defence four quick tricks in this suit.

Tip 42 : If only one card in partner's hand will do to defeat their contract, play partner to hold that card.

(1)	NORTH
Dealer South	♠ K Q 7
Nil vulnerable	♡ J 6
	◇ 8 5 3 2
	♣ A K J 9

EAST
♠ 5 2
♡ A 7 4 3
◇ A K Q 6
♣ 8 7 2

South opened 1NT, 12-14, and North raised to 3NT. West leads the 10 of spades, won by dummy's king. The jack of hearts is led from dummy. How should East plan the defence?

(2)	NORTH
Dealer South	♠ K J 10 6 4
Nil vulnerable	♡ A 5
	◇ K 9 4 2
	♣ Q 10

EAST
♠ A Q 7
♡ J 4 3 2
◇ Q 10 3
♣ A J 8

WEST	NORTH	EAST	SOUTH
			1NT (1)
No	2♡ (2)	No	2♠
No	3NT	All pass	
(1) 12-14	(2) Transfer to spades		

West leads the 4 of clubs, 10 from dummy and East's jack wins. How should East continue?

To become a top defender, you must count the HCP in dummy, add your own and those revealed by declarer in the bidding. Subtract the total from 40 to see what partner can possibly hold.

Solutions

(1) Dummy has 14 HCP, East 13 and declarer has 12 or 13. If declarer has 13 and partner 0, you have no chance. If declarer has 12, partner has one jack and you need to pray it is the ◊J, the only card of any use to you. You must rise with the ace of hearts at trick 2 and switch to the ◊6.

Declarer held :   ♠ A J 4 3   ♥ K Q 10   ◊ 10 7 4   ♣ Q 10 3

If you duck the first heart, declarer can cash out for nine tricks. If you rise with the ace of hearts, you must lead your low diamond. If you start with a top diamond, the suit is blocked when West has J-x.

(2) The thinking here is similar. Dummy has 13 HCP, East has 14 and so South has 12 or 13. If it is 13, you have no chance. If it is 12, partner will hold the jack of diamonds. You have one club trick already and the ♣A and A-Q in spades give you four tricks. To score a fifth trick you need to switch to diamonds at once. The full deal :

NORTH
♠ K J 10 6 4
♥ A 5
◊ K 9 4 2
♣ Q 10

WEST
♠ 8 5 2
♥ 10 8 6
◊ J 8
♣ 9 7 5 4 3

EAST
♠ A Q 7
♥ J 4 3 2
◊ Q 10 3
♣ A J 8

SOUTH
♠ 9 3
♥ K Q 9 7
◊ A 7 6 5
♣ K 6 2

A diamond shift at trick 2 beats 3NT. At the table, East cashed ♣A at trick 2 and led a third club. Counting points would expose the futility of this.

Tip 43 : Beware of setting up winners for declarer if you can score tricks by a different route.

Dealer East   NORTH
Both vulnerable   ♠ A 7 2
                              ♡ 4 3
                              ◊ J 9 7 4 2
                              ♣ 5 4 2

                                            EAST
                                            ♠ 4
                                            ♡ J 10 8
                                            ◊ A K 10 8 3
                                            ♣ K Q 8 6

WEST	NORTH	EAST	SOUTH
		1◊	1♠
2♡ (1)	No	4♡	4♠
Double	No	No	No

(1) Natural, game invitational but not forcing

West leads the 5 of diamonds to East's king, South playing the 6. How should East continue?

This was the full deal :

                              NORTH
                              ♠ A 7 2
                              ♡ 4 3
                              ◊ J 9 7 4 2
                              ♣ 5 4 2
WEST   EAST
♠ K 5   ♠ 4
♡ K Q 9 7 5 2   ♡ J 10 8
◊ 5   ◊ A K 10 8 3
♣ 10 9 7 3   ♣ K Q 8 6
                              SOUTH
                              ♠ Q J 10 9 8 6 3
                              ♡ A 6
                              ◊ Q 6
                              ♣ A J

South has done well to bid 4♠ since it is unlikely that North would find the club lead needed to defeat 4♡. A club to the ace and a club return would allow South to score a club ruff.

Any other lead would enable declarer to succeed. Say North leads a diamond. Dummy wins and a trump is led. South wins and switches to the queen of spades, king, ace. Declarer would ruff the next diamond, play a trump to hand and lead a club to the king and ace. The spade return would be ruffed in dummy followed by dummy's top diamond and a diamond ruff. Now when declarer plays his remaining trumps, North is caught in a show-up squeeze and declarer does not lose a second club.

West's lead of the 5 of diamonds is the lowest possible diamond and is therefore a singleton. The only missing diamond is the queen and with ♢Q-5 West would have led the queen. Therefore South still has the ♢Q.

It is tempting to take your two diamond winners and continue with a third diamond, expecting West to overruff South. This is a poor plan since it sets up dummy's jack of diamonds as a winner. On the actual deal, South would discard a heart on the third diamond, ruffed by West. Later a trump to dummy's ace draws the missing trumps and declarer's club loser would disappear on the jack of diamonds.

It is also possible that West would be unable to overruff declarer. Imagine that declarer started with these cards :

♠ K J 10 9 8 6 3   ♡ K Q   ♢ Q 6   ♣ A J

After ♢K, ♢A and a third diamond, declarer could ruff with the king of spades and then lead the jack of spades, picking up West's queen. The ♠7 in dummy would be an entry later to the jack of diamonds for a club discard. The defence would take only two diamonds and a heart.

East can solve all these problems by continuing with the ♢3 after winning with the ♢K. West will ruff and whether the switch is to the ♡K or a club, declarer has two more losers. East's remaining ♢A-10-8 over dummy's ♢J-9-7 prevents declarer scoring any diamond tricks.

The actual tip, which would have given the show away originally, could usefully be expanded to read :

Tip 43 : If you know partner is void, give partner a ruff rather than cash a winner if the latter play sets up one or more winners for declarer.

Tip 44 : When switching to a suit such as J-x-x or Q-x-x when dummy holds low cards on your right, lead low if you need only two tricks but lead the honour if you need three or more tricks from the suit.

(1)		NORTH	
Dealer West		♠ Q 7	
Nil vulnerable		♡ 4 3 2	
		◊ A Q 10 9 2	
		♣ 5 4 2	

		EAST	
		♠ 4 3	
		♡ A 8 6 5	
		◊ 8 6 4 3	
		♣ J 7 3	

WEST	NORTH	EAST	SOUTH
1♡	No	2♡	4♠
No	No	No	

West leads the queen of hearts, East plays the ace and South drops the king. How should East continue?

(2)		NORTH	
Dealer North		♠ J 7	
Nil vulnerable		♡ 4 3 2	
		◊ A K 10 9	
		♣ 8 6 5 4	

		EAST	
		♠ 4	
		♡ A K J 8 5	
		◊ Q 7 4 2	
		♣ Q 7 3	

WEST	NORTH	EAST	SOUTH
	No	1♡	4♠
No	No	No	

West leads the 7 of hearts, East plays the king and South drops the ten. When East cashes ♡A, South plays ♡Q and West ♡9. What next?

(3)
Dealer South
Nil vulnerable

NORTH
♠ A K 10 7 6 2
♡ 9 8 5
◊ 9 6 2
♣ 4

EAST
♠ 5
♡ J 7 4
◊ A 10 8 7 4
♣ 10 5 3 2

WEST	NORTH	EAST	SOUTH
			1♣
Double	1♠	2◊	3NT
No	No	No	

West leads the queen of diamonds. Plan East's defence.

Solutions

(1) South's ♡K is clearly a singleton, so there are no more tricks there and a glance at dummy will reveal there are no diamond tricks for the defence either. Therefore you need *three* tricks from the clubs and should shift to the jack of clubs. South began with :

    ♠ A K J 10 6 3 2   ♡ K   ◊ J 7   ♣ K 9 8

The ♣J switch beats the contract as West has A-Q-10-6. A low club allows South to play low in hand and make the contract. On any return but a club, South makes twelve tricks.

(2) You have no more tricks coming in hearts and cannot score two from the diamonds. You need two more tricks. Switch to a *low* club and hope South has to guess with a K-J holding. South began with :

    ♠ A K Q 10 9 8 3 2   ♡ Q 10   ◊ 6   ♣ K J

Only a low club at trick 3 gives the defence a chance.

(3) Partner's lead marks South with the ◊K and the bidding indicates that South has a long, strong club suit. You should grab the ◊A and switch to the *jack* of hearts. Nothing else works as South started with :

    ♠ 9 4   ♡ K 6 2   ◊ K 5   ♣ A K Q J 9 8

Tip 45 : If your opening lead can be read as a sure singleton or a possible singleton, partner's card at trick 1 should be taken as a suit preference signal.

(1)
Dealer East
Nil vulnerable

NORTH
♠ K 8 5
♡ Q J 6
◊ K 7
♣ A K Q J 3

WEST
♠ 6 3 2
♡ A 9 8 7
◊ A 9 6 5 3
♣ 2

WEST	NORTH	EAST	SOUTH
		No	2♠ (weak two)
No	4♠	All pass	

West leads the 2 of clubs : Ace - 9 - 7. The ♡6 is played from dummy : 2 from East - King from South. Plan the defence for West.

(2)
Dealer South
Nil vulnerable

NORTH
♠ Q 10 8 6 2
♡ Q 9 6
◊ Q 7 5
♣ Q 5

WEST
♠ K 3
♡ A 8 4 2
◊ 4
♣ K J 10 7 6 3

WEST	NORTH	EAST	SOUTH
			2◊ (weak two)
3♣	3◊	3♠	5◊
Double	No	No	No

West leads the King of spades : 2 - 9 - 5. How should West continue?

(1) Partner's ♣9 cannot rationally be taken as an encouraging signal for clubs or a count card in clubs. Knowing the number of clubs partner holds cannot matter to West.

The *nine* should be read as a suit preference card. Normally this would ask you to play a heart, the high suit excluding trumps. Declarer's play of a heart to the king means that partner cannot possibly want hearts. Exceptionally the high suit here indicates the entry is in trumps. West should take the ♡A and lead a trump. This is essential as declarer's hand is :

♠ Q J 10 9 7 4   ♡ K 10   ◊ Q 8 4   ♣ 10 7

If you fail to lead trumps soon enough declarer can discard a club on the third heart and lose just the three aces.

(2) As partner must have five spades for the 3♠ bid, partner's ♠9 cannot ask you to continue spades. Partner knows that if you could lead another spade, declarer would ruff. The 9 should be taken as a suit preference signal, high card for the high suit, hearts. That also caters for the possibility that your ♠K lead was a singleton. The full deal :

NORTH
♠ Q 10 8 6 2
♡ Q 9 6
◊ Q 7 5
♣ Q 5

♠ K 3	♠ A J 9 7 4
♡ A 8 4 2	♡ K 3
◊ 4	◊ K 8
♣ K J 10 7 6 3	♣ A 9 8 4

SOUTH
♠ 5
♡ J 10 7 5
◊ A J 10 9 6 3 2
♣ 2

En route to winning the 1995 Australian Grand National Teams, David Beauchamp, West, and Ted Chadwick produced a sparkling defence and a stern lesson to South. ♠K lead, East played the nine. ♡2 switch to the king, heart to the ace, *four* of hearts (suit preference for clubs) ruffed by East, *low* club to the king, fourth heart ruffed with the ◊K, +800.

Tip 46 : Often a defender may know more about the layout of a hand than declarer does. Make the most of that information to present declarer with a losing option.

(1)	NORTH		
Dealer South	♠ A 4		
E-W vulnerable	♡ 8 6 5 3		
	◊ A 5 4		
	♣ J 10 9 5		

WEST
♠ Q J 8 5
♡ K 9 4
◊ Q J 2
♣ 7 4 2

WEST	NORTH	EAST	SOUTH
			1♡ (5-card majors)
No	3♡	No	4♡
No	No	No	

West leads the ◊Q, taken by the Ace. East plays the 8 (encouraging). ♡3 from dummy, 7 from East, Queen from South. Plan West's defence.

(2)	NORTH		
Dealer West	♠ A K J		
E-W vulnerable	♡ 9 6		
	◊ K Q J 7 4		
	♣ K 8 2		

EAST
♠ 8
♡ A K J 10 3
◊ 8 6 3 2
♣ 7 6 5

WEST	NORTH	EAST	SOUTH
No	1♣ (1)	2♡ (weak)	2NT
3♡	No	No	3NT
No	No	No	

(1) Artificial, strong

West leads the 2 of hearts (thirds and fifths). Plan East's defence.

(1) As East cannot hold two hearts, the defence has only one trump trick.

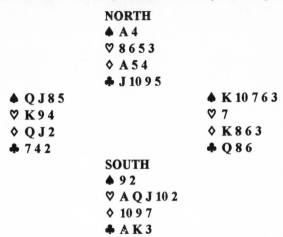

NORTH
♠ A 4
♡ 8 6 5 3
♦ A 5 4
♣ J 10 9 5

♠ Q J 8 5
♡ K 9 4
♦ Q J 2
♣ 7 4 2

♠ K 10 7 6 3
♡ 7
♦ K 8 6 3
♣ Q 8 6

SOUTH
♠ 9 2
♡ A Q J 10 2
♦ 10 9 7
♣ A K 3

If West takes ♡K at once, declarer will use the ♠A entry to take the club finesse, draw trumps, cash the clubs and pitch the spade loser on dummy's fourth club. If West ducks smoothly at trick 1, declarer may believe the heart finesse is working and cross to ♠A entry to lead another heart. Doom.

(2)

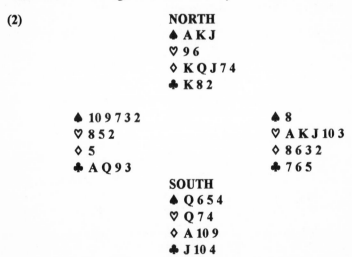

NORTH
♠ A K J
♡ 9 6
♦ K Q J 7 4
♣ K 8 2

♠ 10 9 7 3 2
♡ 8 5 2
♦ 5
♣ A Q 9 3

♠ 8
♡ A K J 10 3
♦ 8 6 3 2
♣ 7 6 5

SOUTH
♠ Q 6 5 4
♡ Q 7 4
♦ A 10 9
♣ J 10 4

East knows South has the ♡Q stopper but South does not know the heart layout. To maximise pressure on South, win with ♡A and return ♡J.

Tip 47 : Spot the Achilles heel.

(1)
Dealer South
E-W vulnerable

NORTH
♠ 8 6 5 4 3
♡ Q J 2
◊ A 5
♣ Q 4 2

WEST
♠ K J 9 7
♡ K 6
◊ 9 6 4
♣ 10 8 5 3

SOUTH	WEST	NORTH	EAST
1NT (1)	No	2♡ (2)	No
2♠	No	2NT	No
3NT	No	No	No

(1) 1NT = 15-17   (2) Transfer to spades

West leads the 3 of clubs and dummy's ♣Q wins. The ♡Q is led : 7 from East and 5 from South. Plan the defence for West.

(2)
Dealer South
N-S vulnerable

NORTH
♠ 9 4
♡ A K 10 9 7
◊ K 8 4 3
♣ 5 3

EAST
♠ K 8 6 5 2
♡ Q 5 4
◊ 7 6
♣ K 7 6

SOUTH	WEST	NORTH	EAST
1♣	No	1♡	No
1♠	No	2◊	No
3NT	No	No	No

West leads ◊J won by South's ace. Declarer now plays the ♡J, 2 from West, 7 from dummy. Plan the defence.

(1) As trick 1 marks South with ♣A-K there is little future in that direction. You should switch but are diamonds or spades your best bet? There are enough points missing to make either suit possible. In diamonds, partner would need to be as good as K-Q-J-x or K-Q-x-x-x.

The spade position is clearer. South's rejection of spades marks South with a doubleton spade and hence partner also has two spades. Give partner the ♠A and the contract can be beaten. Therefore switch to the ♠7 as you need far less from partner there than you do in diamonds where you need partner to have length and strength. South in fact held :

♠ 10 2 ♡ A 10 9 8 ◇ K Q J 3 ♣ A K 9

The Achilles heel tip can be expanded. To have given it earlier would have made problem 1 too simple.

Tip 47 : When dummy's bid suit turns out to be particularly weak, it is often attractive to switch to that suit early in the defence.

After taking the ♠A, East should realise that you want a spade back and not a club, even if South drops the 10 of spades under the ace. East also knows that South started with two spades. If West had ♠J-9-7-2 and did not want a spade return, West would lead the *nine* of spades.

(2) Declarer's diamonds are too good to offer hope there. As South has four spades, even if partner has ♠A-Q you cannot collect enough tricks from spades to beat 3NT. You should switch to the ♣6, not the king - - - see Tip 41 - - - in the hope that declarer's weakness is in clubs. The full deal:

NORTH
♠ 9 4
♡ A K 10 9 7
◇ K 8 4 3
♣ 5 3

WEST	EAST
♠ 10 7	♠ K 8 6 5 2
♡ 8 6 2	♡ Q 5 4
◇ J 10 9 5	◇ 7 6
♣ A Q 9 4	♣ K 7 6

SOUTH
♠ A Q J 3
♡ J 3
◇ A Q 2
♣ J 10 8 2

Tip 48 : If the right defence is clear to you but may not be clear to partner, try to find a way to make it impossible for partner to go wrong.

Dealer West		NORTH	
N-S vulnerable		♠ J	
		♡ 10 9 6	
		◇ A K Q J 7	
		♣ A 9 6 5	

WEST			
♠ 7 5			
♡ K Q 7 3			
◇ 9 5 3 2			
♣ K 4 2			

WEST	NORTH	EAST	SOUTH
No	1◇	2♠ (1)	2NT
No	3NT	All pass	

(1) Weak jump overcall

1. West leads the 7 of spades : Jack - *Queen* - 3.
2. East returns the ♠9 of spades : ♠6 - ♠5 - ♡6 discarded from dummy.
3. East continues with ♠10, South wins ♠A, West and North throw hearts.
4-8 : Five rounds of diamonds follow. East discards ♡4, ♡8 and ♠2. South pitches ♠8, ♡2 and ♣7. What should West discard on the fifth diamond?

Decide on your answer before looking at the complete deal.

		NORTH	
		♠ J	
		♡ 10 9 6	
		◇ A K Q J 7	
		♣ A 9 6 5	
♠ 7 5			♠ K Q 10 9 4 2
♡ K Q 7 3			♡ J 8 4
◇ 9 5 3 2			◇ 10 4
♣ K 4 2			♣ Q 3
		SOUTH	
		♠ A 8 6 3	
		♡ A 5 2	
		◇ 8 6	
		♣ J 10 8 7	

The end-position after eight tricks looks like this :

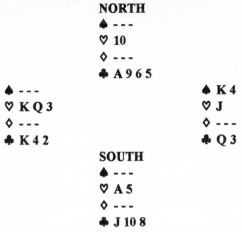

NORTH
♠ - - -
♡ 10
◇ - - -
♣ A 9 6 5

WEST
♠ - - -
♡ K Q 3
◇ - - -
♣ K 4 2

EAST
♠ K 4
♡ J
◇ - - -
♣ Q 3

SOUTH
♠ - - -
♡ A 5
◇ - - -
♣ J 10 8

West still has to make a discard.

Firstly, West should realise that with East having thrown two hearts, declarer will succeed if holding the ♣Q. Imagine South has Q-x-x in the above diagram. Whether West discards a heart or a club, declarer can play ace and another heart to endplay West.

West must therefore assume that East has the ♣Q for which there is strong supporting evidence : East played the *nine* of spades at trick 2, the *ten* of spades at trick 3, and discarded the *two* of spades later. Playing the lowest card each time evinces some interest in the lowest suit.

If East does have the ♣Q, East has a sure entry to the spade winners. That is clear to West but may not be clear to East. To make sure that East does not make a mistake, West should discard the *king* of clubs.

In the final of a National Teams Championship, West discarded the 3 of hearts in the above diagram. Declarer led a low club from dummy and East erred (as partners do) by playing low. The jack forced the king and when the ♣A dropped the queen on the next round, declarer made the contract.

East could have switched to a heart after winning two spades but that is always clearer in the *post mortem* than at the table. West needs to find the solution since the First Law of Defence has to be : 'If a mistake is possible, partner is more than capable of making it.'

Tip 49 : When declarer in no-trumps fails to tackle a good, long suit in dummy, you can be almost certain that the suit is running and will provide declarer with as many tricks as there are cards in that suit.

(1)		**NORTH**	
Dealer East		♠ 8 7 2	
N-S vulnerable		♡ K 6	
		◊ A Q J 10 7 4	
		♣ 10 3	

WEST
♠ A K 4
♡ A 7 3
◊ 9 5
♣ J 9 8 5 2

WEST	NORTH	EAST	SOUTH
		No	1NT (12-14)
No	3NT	All pass	

West leads the 5 of clubs, 3 from dummy and East's king is taken by the ace. Declarer continues with the ♡J. How should West defend?

(2)		**NORTH**	
Dealer South		♠ A 9 6	
N-S vulnerable		♡ Q 2	
		◊ A K Q 8 6	
		♣ K 9 8	

WEST
♠ 10 8 4 3
♡ A J 3
◊ 10 3 2
♣ A 4 2

WEST	NORTH	EAST	SOUTH
			No
No	1◊	No	1NT
No	3NT	All pass	

West leads the 3 of spades : ♠6 - ♠7 - ♠K. South returns the 3 of clubs. How should West plan the defence? If you take the ♣A, what next?

(1) As East's play of the king of clubs denies the queen, South began with ♣A-Q. The failure to tackle diamonds at trick 2 firmly places the ◊K with South. That gives declarer eight tricks and a heart will be the ninth.

The only hope for the defence is for West to rise with the ace of hearts and switch to ♠K, ♠A and a third spade. That will work as South held :

♠ J 9 6 ♡ Q J 4 2 ◊ K 6 3 ♣ A Q 4

(2) East's play of the ♠7 as third-hand-high means that South started with K-Q-J of spades. East would have played the queen or jack if possible. South's club at trick 2 rather than starting on the diamonds means that the diamonds are ready to roll. You can thus count declarer to have three spades and five diamonds. The club will be declarer's ninth trick and so you must take the ♣A at once.

Your only hope is to switch to hearts at trick 3, but which heart?

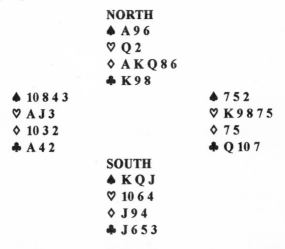

NORTH
♠ A 9 6
♡ Q 2
◊ A K Q 8 6
♣ K 9 8

♠ 10 8 4 3
♡ A J 3
◊ 10 3 2
♣ A 4 2

♠ 7 5 2
♡ K 9 8 7 5
◊ 7 5
♣ Q 10 7

SOUTH
♠ K Q J
♡ 10 6 4
◊ J 9 4
♣ J 6 5 3

In the Open Teams final of the 1995 Asia, Africa and Middle East Championships, won by South Africa, Egypt's Walid El-Ahmady rose with the ace of clubs and switched to the *jack* of hearts, the only card to give the defence a chance. The queen was taken by the king and the ♡7 came back. Declarer would have succeeded by playing low but, reasonably enough, he rose with the 10. Curtains!

At the other table the Egyptian declarer made ten tricks for +13 IMPs.

Tip 50 : Always consider the implications when partner's honour card as third-hand-high denies the next lower card.

Dealer North	**NORTH**		
Nil vulnerable	♠ Q 6		
	♡ 6 2		
	◊ K 10 6 5 3 2		
	♣ J 6 3		

WEST
♠ A 9 7 5 3 2
♡ A Q 8 5 3
◊ 8
♣ 2

WEST	NORTH	EAST	SOUTH
	No	No	1♣
1♠	No	No	1NT
2♡	3◊	No	3NT
No	No	No	

West leads the 5 of hearts, East plays the 10 and South wins with the jack. South continues with the 4 of spades, low from West and dummy's queen wins. On the next spade East follows and South plays the king. How should West plan the defence?

Solution

There are two important clues :

(1) When playing third-hand-high with touching cards, it is standard to play cheapest of the touching cards. From 10-9 or 10-9-x in third seat, East would play the 9 when playing third-hand-high. It follows that East's play of the ♡10 denies the ♡9 and so South started with at least K-J-9 in hearts. Therefore, you cannot gain by cashing the ♡A.

(2) Declarer's failure to tackle diamonds means the diamonds are ready to run (see Tip 49). Declarer will have at least A-Q-x in diamonds.

You must shift to a club, hoping East has the ace and can lead a heart through declarer's remaining K-9. South started with :

♠ K J 4   ♡ K J 9   ◊ A Q 9   ♣ K Q 7 5